M000076145

JUMPSTART
your
LEADERSHIP

JUMPSTART
your
LEADERSHIP

—10 JOLTS—
TO LEVERAGE
YOUR LEADERSHIP

SHAWN DOYLE

© Copyright 2013—Shawn Doyle

All rights reserved. This book is protected by the copyright laws of the United States of America. This book may not be copied or reprinted for commercial gain or profit. The use of short quotations or occasional page-copying for personal or group study is permitted and encouraged. Permission will be granted upon request.

Sound Wisdom
167 Walnut Bottom Road
Shippensburg, PA 17257

www.soundwisdom.com

This book and all other Sound Wisdom books are available at bookstores and distributors worldwide.

ISBN 13: 978-1-937879-20-4

ISBN Ebook: 978-1-937879-23-5

For Worldwide Distribution, Printed in the U.S.A.

1 2 3 4 5 6 7 / 17 16 15 14 13

DEDICATION

This book is dedicated with the utmost respect and admiration to the best leader I have ever reported to, Mr. Filemon Lopez. There are leaders and there are managers— Filemon is a true and gifted leader, who changes lives. I know because mine was once one of them.

CONTENTS

JUMPSTART YOUR LEADERSHIP

"Love and respect do not automatically accompany a position of leadership. They must be earned."

—AUTHOR UNKNOWN

HELLO, and welcome to *Jumpstart Your Leadership*. Are your jumper cables ready? Are they hooked up to your leadership battery? Over the last 23 years, I have conducted countless leadership programs and have delivered keynote speeches for corporations and companies both small and large. I have seen many different situations, and have heard lots of leadership nightmare stories. To be blunt, there is one thing that I'm still amazed by: leaders in many organizations still lack basic leadership competence. Even more astoundingly, companies often don't see what is missing!

I'm glad that you decided to join me in this journey through *Jumpstart Your Leadership*. I am excited because I'm convinced that if you take this material and apply it, you will see dramatic changes and a jolt in your leadership skills. Even more exciting are the results that you will see as a leader working with your team. In short, you can become *the leader*. You know what I mean; you know the one—the person whom everyone *wants* to work with, the rare and special leader who inspires and motivates the team. You can be that leader. Really, I just know it.

Why did I decide to write this book? I wrote this book because I want to make a difference in the world and because I see many leaders who are struggling with leadership. As a result, they're very frustrated.

In many organizations, people are promoted to leadership positions as a result of *technical* competence. These people are, of course, thrilled to be promoted. However, in many cases they soon realize that *technical* competence does not necessarily equal *leadership* competence. Herein lies the problem. They will not admit that they don't know how to lead, since that may be seen as a sign of weakness—no one wants to admit not knowing something. As a result, they continue to struggle, because most companies don't provide any appropriate leadership development.

The companies that these leaders work for have made a huge strategic error, because they assume that the person who got promoted has the talent and ability to lead, to manage, and to supervise. This approach hasn't worked well in the past, and it doesn't work well today. What's the solution? One of the main solutions is to teach leaders core concepts and then train them to apply those concepts. This leads to a massive increase in leadership effectiveness—and more importantly, results.

Justin Jones was a brilliant and talented member of the IT team. He was a great worker who got along well with everyone. After a few years at the company, the effectiveness and speed of Justin's work had been noticed by the right people, so he was promoted and given a team of 16 people reporting to him. When Justin got promoted, he was thrilled and initially excited about the work and the opportunity. However, not long after his promotion, he began to have problems. A couple of people on his team could not stand one another and were constantly arguing. One team member suffered from a low level of confidence, while another team member was painfully and clearly incompetent. They needed to be fired. Justin hadn't realized what he'd gotten himself into. He recognized that he needed training in leadership skills and techniques. Still, he did not want to admit to his company that he didn't know what he was doing. He was afraid that he would be instantly demoted and humiliated, forced to go back to his old job. So what did Justin do? He adopted the "classic" technique: He decided that the best approach was to lead people the way *his manager led him*. After all, his manager was successful, right? His manager had been promoted and was well perceived in the company as hard-nosed and results-oriented.

By the way, this isn't a true story—Justin is a fictional character. Keep in mind, though, that every day throughout the world, there are people promoted to leadership positions who share Justin's pain. Think about the problems that are inherent in the Justins of the world. We have managers who lack confidence because they don't know how to lead. We have team members who are frustrated because they are reporting to managers who don't know how to lead. We have managers who are emulating the behaviors of bad managers whom they've worked with over the years. This is an invitation for disaster, because we have the blind leading the seeing, the unskilled leading the skilled. This leads to high levels of frustration and low morale in many organizations.

In this book, I've boiled down what I know about leadership. This is based on some 23 years of research and experience, both as a leader and as a coach and trainer of leaders throughout the corporate world. Think of them as "jolts" to your leadership battery. I have deliberately left this book short and sweet because I know that everyone is time-challenged; but don't confuse quantity with quality! Understand that if you apply these concepts, you will be successful. The results that you get may even surprise you!

In a nutshell, these are the 10 jolts that we're going to cover:

JOLT #1:
HAVE A MISSION AND VISION STATEMENT.

In this chapter, I will review with you some important reasons why your organization needs to have a mission and vision statement to be effective. More broadly, I'll outline why having a mission and vision statement will lead to your increased effectiveness in leading the team toward a destination—and the destination is success.

JOLT #2:
HAVE A SHORT-, MID-, AND LONG-TERM PLAN.

Here you go! I will give you the critical tools and techniques for developing plans that look beyond today, tomorrow, this month, and this quarter. In order to lead people effectively, you have to be able to create strategies and solid plans so that your team can help generate the results. I will show you how to put together short-, mid-, and long-term plans.

JOLT #3:
HIRE PEOPLE SMARTER THAN YOU.

The best, most talented leaders are generalists: people who know how to hire specialists with expertise in their respective areas. In this chapter, I will tell you how to do just that.

JOLT #4:
COMMUNICATE WITH ALL TEAM MEMBERS.

Leaders need to be skilled communicators and communicate regularly and frequently with everyone on the team so that everyone feels acknowledged and appreciated. In this chapter, I will give you approaches and strategies to help you create a high-level communication culture that builds morale and reduces turnover.

JOLT #5:
CREATE A MOTIVATIONAL ENVIRONMENT.

The most frequent question I get from leaders is, "How in the world do I motivate these folks?" Since this seems to be a key issue, I think it is important for you to understand how to create a motivational environment that encourages a team to work at a higher level, increases morale, and most importantly, improves results. In this chapter, I will give you all the elements you need to create this kind of environment.

JOLT #6:
REWARD EXCEPTIONAL PERFORMERS.

In many cases, I hear managers say that they are constrained by policies and procedures and can't reward team members for exceptional performances. Policies and procedures can seem to raise barriers, but often these barriers do not actually exist. Sure, specific human resources policies must be followed. However, this does not mean that you *can't* reward for an exceptional performance. When employees perform at an exceptional level, they become frustrated and demoralized when they get minimal rewards. Therefore, it is up to you as the leader to design methods and tactics for rewarding a truly exceptional job performance. This will allow you to retain exceptional team members by rewarding them appropriately. In this chapter, I will outline ideas and techniques for rewarding your champions.

JOLT #7:
HOLD PEOPLE ACCOUNTABLE
FOR THEIR WORK.

The biggest flaw that I see in leaders is their lack of willingness to hold people accountable for their work. Many times, when I get calls from prospective clients, they want me to come in and "fix" a problem—a problem that has been created by a manager who has not held people accountable. The real problems in these situations are the managers who do not have the courage to provide honest feedback. Is there a specific methodology for providing feedback that is both diplomatic and appropriate? Yes. I see leaders who are not providing feedback of the correct type. The reason is that, quite simply, they're afraid of conflict and of the reaction they might get. In this case, to be quite blunt, they should not be in leadership roles. In this chapter, I will show you how to hold people accountable in a way that is both diplomatic and effective.

JOLT #8:
COMMIT TO THE INDIVIDUAL DEVELOPMENT
OF EVERY TEAM MEMBER.

Leaders have an obligation to provide employees with the development that they deserve. By the way, this includes every member of the team—not only the salespeople and managers, but also administrative staff and others who might not normally be considered "developmental material."

In this chapter, I will show you how to shatter the myth of the "dead-end job."

JOLT #9:
TELL THE STORY CONSISTENTLY AND REPEATEDLY.

I have had the privilege of observing many presentations by CEOs, presidents, and CFOs of Fortune 500 companies. I have also had the unique opportunity to see them give the same presentation to different groups. What I find remarkable when I see these folks in action is that they tell the same story consistently and repeatedly. When this is done, and done well, the message starts to get across to all team members. Like a good campfire story, it is repeated among the ranks and becomes a vital part of the corporate culture. In this chapter, I will cover ideas and approaches to becoming a powerful storyteller as a leader.

JOLT #10:
ALWAYS BE HONEST AND AUTHENTIC.

Many of the latest and greatest leadership books tout the power of authenticity. I couldn't agree more! Authenticity is certainly a crucial part of being an effective leader. When you're not being honest and you're not being authentic, people can tell. This means that you need to speak to team members openly and honestly, and—even though you are part of a corporate culture or organization—you still have to be who you are. In this chapter, I will cover how to be successful and still be you.

Those are The 10 Jolts of Leadership that I'll be covering. Before you read further, I want to ask you a favor. I want you to read this book differently. I want you to read every page of this book and as you read it think about these questions:

- Do I possess the qualities covered in this jolt?

- Is this particular jolt one of my strengths or is there room for improvement?

- Is this an area that I have addressed before?

- What difference would it make if I applied these principles to my leadership skills and abilities?

- What impact would these ideas have on my team?

- Do I think that each of these concepts is important?

- Am I willing to apply effort toward improving in these specific areas?

At the end of each chapter you will find a Work it page. This section is designed to help you stop and think about what you just read. It will help you determine your strengths and the areas you need improvement. It will also allow you to take notes and to create action plans to build on each foundation.

I do know one thing: Leadership development is not an event; it is a process. The leaders that I see who are successful are leaders who are committed to their own growth and development. When leaders commit to their own growth and development, they're motivated, enthusiastic, and energized.

Now you have a choice. Will you embrace these concepts and change your leadership skills for life, or will you read this book just to say you've read it, to check it off your list? It's up to you. Only you can be your own architect and decide to lay the foundation for your leadership future.

CHAPTER 1

JOLT #1:
HAVE A MISSION AND VISION STATEMENT

"The energy, the faith, the devotion which we bring this endeavor will light our bounty and all who serve it, and the glow from that fire can truly light the world."
—JOHN F. KENNEDY

ONE of the critical elements of successful leadership is having a mission and vision statement for the organization, for the team, and even for individuals (which we'll discuss more later). I see many organizations that have their mission and vision statement proudly displayed on a marble plaque in their lobby. They use it as a signature at the end of each email. Some of the leaders in these organizations actually follow the mission and vision statement and internalize its values. In other organizations, the mission and vision statement just takes up space on the wall. It truly has no meaning. When you ask employees what the mission and vision statement of their organization is, some are able to recite it verbatim, while others look like a deer caught in the headlights, or mumble like Dustin Hoffman in *Rainman*.

Before we begin an in-depth discussion about mission and vision statements, we need to look at the definitions of *mission* and *vision*. More importantly, we need to find out what mission *really* means.

The official Merriam-Webster's dictionary definition of "mission" is "a pre-established and often self-imposed objective or purpose." I think there are a few interesting aspects of this definition. One important element of the definition is the word *pre-established*. It indicates that there has been some forethought, and that some thought went into the establishment of a mission. Secondly, I think that the word *self-imposed* is notable. This word clearly indicates that the creation of a mission is a proactive activity, as opposed to a reactive activity. The last two important words in the definition are *objective* and *purpose*. Obviously, in business, there must be objectives to meet. Objectives enable us to make sales, increase profitability, and increase cash flow. Clearly, then, mission and vision statements do help organizations reach goals by establishing and "self-imposing" them.

We also need to look carefully at the definition of "vision" (again from Merriam-Webster), which is "the act or power of imagination, the mode of seeing or conceiving, or unusual discernment or foresight."

Notice the definition's acknowledgement of the power of imagination and its use of the word *foresight*. Isn't it true that great leaders should have a powerful imagination and great foresight? Didn't Walt Disney? Steve Jobs? Mary Kay? If we can agree that great leaders must have the ability to meet objectives and accomplish purposes, as well as have imagination and foresight—or the ability to look at the big picture—then we can all agree that mission and vision are crucial to the success of a leader.

To clarify mission and vision just a little further, I think they are the perfect combination to form an organization's guiding statement. The mission communicates "where we are" and the objectives that we're going to achieve. The vision communicates what we're striving to accomplish long-term, or "where we're headed." In my consulting practice, I have seen companies that are highly successful because they have a well-articulated mission and vision statement, and because they're passionate about putting it into action.

As an added bonus, many organizations add a list of values to their mission and vision statement. Often, there are between four and seven of these values, and each is defined. This list of additional information shows that the organization holds specific values sacred, allows it to hold employees accountable, and encourages the employees to embody these values in the day-to-day operation of the company.

Often you see on this list words like integrity, honesty, ethics, creativity, hard work, family appreciation, etc. The hope is that employees connect with the list and understand that they're working for an organization that shares their values. (For the rest of this chapter, I will refer to mission and vision statements as M/V statements.)

THE BENEFITS OF M/V STATEMENTS

M/V statements are valuable. Here are five benefits to having them:

Increased Focus

In a fast-paced corporate environment, it is very important to stay focused. I have seen many employees come to a company energized about both the work and the opportunity. However, these employees often become jaded when they find out that the great company they signed up to work for doesn't really have a focus. When properly executed, M/V statements allow both the organization and the team to be remarkably focused on future objectives.

Raised Morale

In all the organizations I have seen, the employees of companies that have a well-articulated M/V statement have significantly higher morale than the employees of companies without one. Why is that? Having a M/V statement allows the team to have a rallying cry. It's analogous to a sports team having a cheer, or a traveler having a map. When people are excited about their future possibilities because they know their objectives, their organization's morale goes up. When they do not know their objectives, and therefore are unclear about the future, morale can dip and stay down.

Enhanced Decision-Making

It is easier to make decisions if the team can refer back to an M/V statement. If employees have to make an immediate decision about a customer, product, or procedure, they can refer back to the M/V statement and ask themselves, "Does this tie in with our mission? Will it help us move closer toward our long-term vision?"

You Will Become the Employer of Choice

Companies that have strongly defined M/V statements tend to attract candidates who are smarter, more enthusiastic, and better overall. Certainly Toyota, Virgin, Starbucks, Microsoft, Zappos, and Disney are great examples of multinational companies that have a very clear M/V statement. As a result, they have amazing employees.

Strategic Clarity

When companies have a specific M/V statement, they're able to have clarity about developing and executing a strategy. This is because they can ask themselves, "Is this strategy aligned with our M/V statement or not?" It forces them to look at strategy through different lenses.

WHAT TO DO IF YOU ALREADY HAVE ONE

If you already have an M/V statement somewhere within your organization, then you're one step ahead. So what now? I think the first step to take is to ask some very serious questions about your current M/V statement, as well as your values:

Where Is It?

If your organization has an M/V statement, where is it? I'm not necessarily talking about where it is physically, but rather where it actually is in terms of being adopted and woven into the fabric of the organization. I have seen many organizations that have their M/V statement printed on glossy paper, or included in their annual report. But that is as far as they've gotten. No one in a leadership role is actualizing it. Having an M/V statement sitting in each employee's drawer, never referred to or acted on, and never influencing how the company is run, has absolutely no value. In fact, it might as well not even exist. As a leader, you really need to examine and assess where you are in terms of how aligned the current organization is with the M/V statement. I once worked as a consultant for an organization that already had a well-written M/V statement in place. It had been developed at corporate headquarters, but the team members in the field did not know about it and had decided to create their own. To make matters worse, within the division there were over a dozen separate areas, and each area had its own statement. This created a situation in which the team did not feel like a team, because, to use a sports analogy, players were not playing from the same playbook—and in fact, they all had different plays. They could not figure out why they didn't feel like a team.

Who Knows It?

As a leader, it's very important to identify who knows about the M/V statement. Is it known at headquarters, at the divisional level, or at an individual office level?

Is It Operational?

Are the mission, vision, and values operational? Quite simply, are the words, ideas, and values expressed being put to work in each area of the company (i.e., marketing, sales, shipping, finance)? This is something you need to determine. On a scale of 1 to 100, how well would you say your organization "operational-izes" the M/V statement? I recently stayed at the Red Rocks Casino and Resort in Las Vegas, Nevada. I must say that I found the resort impressive in many ways, including the employees' treatment toward me as a guest, the condition of the property, and the unique design of the architecture, which was clearly meant to provide an amazing, positive customer experience. When I arrived in my room, I noticed a small table placard sitting on top of one of the dressers. It began with the title "A 3" in bold letters. Below that, it read: "Welcome to the Red Rocks Resort and Casino. Our mission is A 3, which means any time, any place, anywhere. As a guest of our hotel, tell us what you need—any time, any place, anywhere, and we will make it happen." I thought this was brilliant, because it is obviously tied in with the resort's mission of customer service. The management was articulating A 3 to both their guests and their employees at the same time.

TRANSLATING MISSION AND VISION AND VALUES

I often see situations in which M/V and values statements are developed at headquarters, but because the local employees are not involved, they feel disconnected from the statement. An employee in the North may feel disconnected because the M/V statement was created in the South in a glass office building. Whose fault is that? The executives are obviously at fault for not communicating and driving their statement throughout the ranks, but perhaps the people even more at fault are the leaders at the local level. It is up to these leaders to translate the mission, vision, and values from an international level to a national level to a local level, taking care that they make sense and have relevance.

First, let's look at the corporate and national M/V statement. If this already exists, does it in exist in writing? Perhaps you can download it from the corporate website. You can also ask the communications department or human resources department if it is available on posters, coffee mugs, mouse pads, etc. In many cases, lots of great promotional materials are created when an M/V statement is first rolled out, but they end up sitting somewhere in storage. Find out whether any exist and how you can get them. It is now up to you to make sure that everyone knows and understands the mission, vision, and values from corporate headquarters—and knows them well. Once the M/V statement is in place, clearly communicated, and well understood, you're ready to move to the next level.

Now look at the division or area M/V statement. Should the division or area statement be exactly the same as the national one? I believe that the M/V statement on a division or area level should be the same or similar. However, it does not hurt to customize it somewhat for a specific location. What is damaging is when the local statement is completely different from the company-wide one. That makes the division or area seem like a separate company, and does not foster a sense of teamwork on a national level. You might legitimately ask at this point, "If I work in the western part of the country, why does it matter whether my employees feel like they're part of a national team? All that should really matter is the fact that they feel like they're part of our regional or area team, right?" Well, smart question—but I couldn't disagree more. Most employees want to feel that they're part of something larger and greater than they are. People want to feel that they *belong* to something. They take pride in affiliation. When people feel that they belong to something larger, that they're working for the greater good, they tend to be more productive and have a higher level of morale and pride.

When you have the division and area M/V statement in place, and it's clearly communicated and well understood, then you're ready to move to the next level—which is often ignored and misunderstood.

Take a look at the *team* M/V statement. The leader (working with the national and division or area statement) works to craft a team M/V statement. Let's use the example of the marketing department. A marketing department may not be specifically connected to the national M/V statement. So the goal of the leader who heads up the marketing department should be to create an M/V statement that aligns with and *complements* the national mission and vision. Let's say I own a cellular phone company. For this example, let's say that our M/V statement is:

> Big Bang Boyz (B3) Communications delivers world-class service with world-class technology for smart customers, and in the future will be the source for communication products and services worldwide.

Notice that there is no specific reference to marketing in the national M/V statement. So it is up to marketing to create an M/V statement that helps *support* world-class service and technology serving world-class customers. We'll have an M/V statement that is specific and relevant *for that department* and for that team. This will also eliminate the attitude expressed by, "Hey, why bother? This has nothing to do with me." Once the team M/V statements are in place, well-articulated, and understood, you're ready to go on.

Now, what the smart leader will do is translate the M/V statement so it can be used to measure individual performance and contributions. So every employee review will contain a segment that scores the employee's job performance against the *national* mission and vision, the *area* mission and vision, and the *team* mission and vision. When individuals are held accountable to contribute toward accomplishing objectives and achieving a specific future, then the M/V statement seriously will no longer be just a piece of paper. It is up to you as the leader to decide how much weight this segment should have in an employee review process. Honestly, if it's not part of the review, then mission, vision, and values really don't have much relevance or importance within your organization.

LEADING THE MISSION AND VISION

Here are five tips for making sure as a leader that you're living the mission and vision every day in your organization:

Live It

Here is something that shocks many of the participants in my leadership programs. As employees go about their day-to-day activities, they are *watching you* as a leader in *everything* that you say and do. Hence, leaders need to be very aware of their behaviors and their actions, because they should be modeling the tenets and philosophy of their M/V statement. They should also at all times be modeling the values of their organization. If they are not, there's a huge philosophical disconnect between what is being said and what is being done—and that is not great leadership; it is dishonest leadership. Because of this, you have to be constantly aware of your behavior and model what you want your employees to emulate at all times.

11

Communicate It Frequently

In one organization I used to work for, every meeting began with a reading of the corporate credo. This, by the way, was not just an empty exercise. The credo was read with reverence and respect and served to remind every employee of the mission, vision, and values of the organization. This is a great example of frequency of communication. As a leader, you have to figure out how to frequently tie specific business situations *back* to the mission, vision, and values, to reinforce them and to teach them. There are many effective communication methods that can be used to continuously communicate the mission and vision. Speeches and meetings, newsletters, websites, email signatures, and printed materials can all be used to reinforce aspects of the mission, vision, and values in their entirety. I have seen leaders use various communication tools to constantly reinforce the message over time so that it eventually becomes woven into the fabric of the organization.

Push It

Most of the great leaders that I see around the country are constantly pushing their M/V statement. On specific projects, they ask, "How does this relate to our mission and vision?" They're always looking for ways to push and reinforce the M/V statement, remind their team members about it, and establish its importance and relevance. This helps employees find ways to apply it to their work.

Hold Others Accountable to It, Too

Great leaders hold their employees accountable to their mission, vision, and values. That means that when they're reviewing the results of a project, they ask specific employees whether the project reflects the true mission and vision of the organization

Weave It into the Fabric of the Organization

As leaders work on different projects, they constantly strive to weave the mission, vision, and values into everything that they do. If they're giving a speech to a group, they mention them. If they're working on a project, they figure out how to weave a reference to them into the project. The goal, of course, is to get the team to a place where they start telling the stories and reinforcing the mission, vision, and values the same way the leader does. That is when the M/V statement has become part of the organization's culture.

WHAT TO DO IF YOU DON'T HAVE A MISSION, VISION, AND VALUES STATEMENT

If you don't have an M/V and values statement, it's now up to you to create one. At this point, some clients will invariably say, "Well—I can't create one, because I'm part of a large organization, and my company doesn't have one." It doesn't matter whether your company doesn't have one or whether it's going to provide one in the future. Just get busy, Boss. The most important leadership quality is being proactive. So if your company does not have an M/V statement, it's simply up to you to create one. As the old saying goes, "It's easier to ask for forgiveness than it is to get permission." Besides, imagine the impact your accomplishment may have if the person you report to finds out that you were smart and proactive enough to get together with your team and create an M/V statement. Hmm, very impressive.

So all of this raises a very big question: How do you get started? Here are four suggested steps to help you create a mission and vision statement.

HOW TO CREATE A MISSION
AND VISION STATEMENT

I am going to strongly suggest that your M/V statement should not be developed by the executive team, but hammered out in a meeting with several people—ideally a meeting in which each functional team is represented. This way you will get "buy-in" and better results, because different people will have helped and added their perspective.

Prepare for the Meeting

You need to prepare for the meeting by determining:

- the specific objectives of the meeting

- where you want to have the meeting

- whom you want to invite

- whether it is convenient for everyone to attend

These are details that need to be thought through carefully. The biggest liability that I've seen with people in leadership roles is that they do not plan their meetings carefully enough and do not give enough forethought to the long-term results of their meetings.

Gather Cross-Functional Teams

When planning the meeting, carefully consider who should attend. As mentioned before, your goal should be to make sure that team members come from many areas in the organization. For example, have people from sales, marketing, finance, operations, engineering, etc. Additionally, if you have offices in different regions of the country, you'll want to have people representing each geographic area in order to create the ideal mix. The reason it's important to have cross-functional teams is twofold: First, when you have an ideal mix of functions and geography, you will get better results. Second, as mentioned before, if you have a cross-functional team, you're much more likely to get better buy-in to the new M/V statement, because a cross section of the organization was involved in formulating it. The last thing you want people to say is that the M/V statement was created without their involvement. Then they'll feel that it has been thrust upon them without their consent.

Select a Facilitator

Ideally, you should not facilitate the meeting yourself. The person you select to facilitate the meeting may or may not be an employee of your company. For instance, you may have someone in your training department who is qualified to facilitate this meeting. You may also want to seriously consider hiring a qualified facilitator from outside your company who has had experience facilitating M/V statement workshops. This requires a certain level of finesse and expertise. Outside facilitators offer several advantages, such as a third-party objective opinion and a reputation as an expert.

Have an Outline

Generally speaking, I have found that it takes two days for a group to work through a mission, vision, and values session, as long as it is well structured, organized, and facilitated.

COMMUNICATION OF THE MISSION, VISION, AND VALUES

Whether you have just developed an M/V and values statement or already had one, it is critically important for you to develop a strategic plan for communicating it to the organization. This plan should contain short-, mid-, and long-term strategies for making sure the statement continues to live within the organization. Here are a few questions you may want to ask yourself while developing this plan:

How Will the Mission Be Communicated?

Will it be communicated via email, video conference, teleseminar, meetings, or brochures?

How Often Does the Mission Need to Be Communicated in Order to Be Effective?

As the leader, only you can answer this question for your organization. I can tell you, though, that most organizations seem to have a remarkably short attention span, which is why you need to have a short-, mid-, and long-term plan for communication.

How Will You Tailor the Communication Plan for Each Level?

Next, determine how the communication plan will be shaped for C-level executives, director-level employees, manager-level employees, supervisors, and frontline employees.

How Will It Be Communicated to External Customers?

How will you communicate your organization's mission, vision, and values to customers, vendors, partners, affiliates, and others?

At this point, you may be saying, "We already have an M/V statement, and it's been in place for a while. This communication plan seems entirely unnecessary." You may be right, and if that's the case, you're in good shape. However, I have seen many companies with an M/V statement that was stale, out of date, or never really got traction to begin with. Other companies have one, but no one knows it. In that case, it is up to you to decide what to do to reinvigorate and reenergize your statement. How much time and energy you want to put into that effort is your call. I can tell you that great

17

leaders use this tool daily to reinvigorate teams and get them to rally around central concepts that everyone can believe in and execute.

I will close this chapter with a quote from Mary Parker Follet, an author and education reformer from the 1920s, who wrote:

> "This is pre-eminently the leadership quality—the ability to organize all the forces there are in an enterprise and make them serve a common purpose. Men [and women] with this ability create a group power rather than express a personal power."

In the next chapter, we will address the importance of short-, mid- and long-term planning.

WORK IT

Does your organization have a mission and vision statement?

_____

_____

_____

_____

If you have one, does everyone on your team know what it is?

_____

_____

_____

Do you have a region/division mission and vision statement?

_____

_____

_____

_____

Do you have a team mission and vision statement?

_____

_____

_____

_____

_____

What do you need to work on regarding mission and vision? Write down your action items.

_____

_____

_____

_____

_____

_____

_____

_____

_____

CHAPTER 2

JOLT #2:
HAVE A SHORT-, MID-,
AND LONG-TERM PLAN

*"When you're dying of thirst, it's too late to
think about digging a well."*
—JAPANESE PROVERB

LET'S take a look at the dictionary definition of *leader*. Merriam-Webster's dictionary defines "leader" as follows:

> **2 :** a person who <u>leads</u> : as **a : <u>GUIDE</u>, <u>CONDUC-</u>
> <u>TOR</u> b** (1) : a person who directs a military force or
> unit (2) : a person who has commanding authority or influence **c** (1) : the principal officer of a
> British political party (2) : a party member chosen
> to manage party activities in a legislative body (3) :
> such a party member presiding over the whole legislative body when the party constitutes a majority
> **d** (1) : <u>CONDUCTOR</u> c (2) : a first or principal performer of a group

21

Notice how this definition of a leader includes words like *lead, guide, correct, manage,* and *conduct*. What I find fascinating is the fact that the idea of planning is not contained *anywhere* within the definition. I am fascinated, but not surprised. Why not? It's quite simple. The one problem that I have found most prevalent in leaders is that most do not have well-articulated and well-developed plans—*if they have any plans at all*. This is shocking.

When I ask most leaders about their one-year plan, their answers are usually fairly clear. Most have one; some do not. Those who have one have a plan for revenue, cash flow profitability, and other areas of the business. The result, however, is quite different when I ask about two- and three-year plans and especially about five-year plans. When I ask for a five-year plan, I get confused looks, mumbled statements, and excuses. Keep in mind that people want and need to be led. The only way that they can be led effectively is if the people leading them have a plan that they can articulate. So let me ask you: Could you clearly articulate your short-, mid-, and long-term plans for your team? If you hesitate in answering this question, welcome to this chapter! In my mind, one of the most critical aspects of leadership is having a long-term plan.

Why It Matters

Your team expects you to be the compass for your organization. That means that when they ask a question, ask for a decision, or need clarification, you must be pointing in the right direction. You won't be able to point them in the right direction unless you know what direction the organization is headed. Having a short-, mid-, and long-term plan in place will help dramatically increase your confidence in the decisions you are making. Early in my career, I worked for an organization that clearly did not have plans for anything beyond day-to-day and week-to-week concerns, and I couldn't believe that they were successful in spite of themselves. I often wondered how successful they would have been if there had been comprehensive short-, mid-, and long-term plans in place. My guess is that they would have done far better.

Research has shown that most people don't have goals on a personal level. Motivational speaker Cynthia Kersey interviewed hundreds of people for her book, *Unstoppable*, and found that most of them did not have goals or plans. She was shocked to discover that only 3 percent of the folks interviewed had goals and only 1 percent had them in writing. If this is the case (and my personal experience with thousands of students across the United States, Canada, and the UK indicates that it is) then we, as leaders, need to help fill the void—at least by having a plan for the team at work. Who knows? Maybe when they find better-disciplined planning at work, it will inspire them to create plans for their lives at home!

There are many benefits to planning:

Decision-Making

When you have plans in place, your decisions will become much easier. You will be able to ask yourself the simple question, "Does this activity, product, or procedure align with our long-term plans or not?" If it does not, then your decision will be fairly simple.

Clarity

When long-term plans are in place, they dramatically increase clarity of communication about goals, because the plans have been thought out and can then be well articulated and well communicated. This allows for less confusion and ambiguity within your organization.

Inspiration

When concrete, well-articulated plans are in place, there is something for teams to be inspired by. As gymnast Mary Lou Retton once said, "Everyone has something they want to get fired up about. Our goal is to identify it, light it, and keep it lit."

Credibility

When having discussions with your team, you will be much more credible if you have specific goals. When discussing items with your boss, peers, colleagues, vendors, and suppliers, you will have much more credibility. Let's face it: No one likes to see a leader who has no direction—that's like a boat without a rudder.

SHORT-TERM PLANNING

Let's start with short-term planning. There are several aspects of short-term planning that you need to consider:

Definition of the Short-Term

I think in the fast-paced world we live in today, short term should be defined as around six months. There are those who argue with me and say 12, but I don't think we live in that kind of society now. What you need to determine is what you need to *accomplish* in the next six months, which is around 180 days or 24 weeks.

In Writing

All planning should be done in writing for several very important reasons. First, all research shows that you are much more likely to accomplish plans that are in writing. Second, when you need to talk to people about the plans, you'll be able to show them a document to reinforce and review concepts. Third, information will be available for both electronic and paper distribution for team members to receive and review. I could actually write an entire book about why plans should be in writing, but you wouldn't buy a book called *Why Things Should Be in Writing*, so enough said.

Categories

Next you should decide what categories you want to have written plans for. Some examples of categories are finances, sales, cash flow, product development, technology, employee development, human resources, revenue, and other. It is entirely up to you to decide what the categories should be in terms of planning and measurement. Some of these may be tied to your company values.

Measurable

All plans when you create them should be specific and measurable and should be able to answer the question, "How will we know that this was achieved?" Then each activity can be planned against its level of effectiveness compared to the metrics for measurement.

MID-TERM PLANNING

The next area to think about is mid-term planning. I see many people in leadership roles who are so worried about today, tomorrow, this week, and this quarter that they do not have the time to sit down and plan for the mid-term. I often wonder whether the American car companies with their short-term thinking ever considered the possibility of an increase in fuel prices and how it would affect the automotive-buying public.

I define mid-term planning as a time frame of the next 12 to 18 months. Again, the mid-term plan should be in writing, well articulated, and well defined. One technique you may want to consider, that could help you a great deal in mid-term planning, is a SWOT analysis. This analysis simply examines the strengths, weaknesses, opportunities, and threats (SWOT) that are present in your industry and on your team. When you are forced to do this analysis of your industry and team, you will recognize areas where improvement is needed and then can plan accordingly. There are needs that can go into the mid-term planning that need to be strengthened. The question you should ask yourself is simply, "Where do we want to be in 12 to 18 months?" This is a very powerful question. By the way, some leaders tell me that they're waiting for their company's official planning time to do this activity. Don't wait. In fact, if you wait, it may never happen. Be one of the first to develop a mid-term plan in your organization. Look, the reality is that being proactive can't hurt. Imagine having a conversation with your manager about specific issues, and being able to refer to the mid-term plan, and, if necessary, produce it on paper. That would certainly give the impression that you are a pro.

One other thing that you may want to consider is making your team a part of the mid-term planning process. This is not to say that what they decide will be the ultimate answer. You will make the final decisions. However, if two heads are better than one, using the new math, ten must be better than one. Tap into the collective intelligence of your respective teams and they will feel motivated and appreciated. When the final mid-term plan rolls out, they will feel that they were part of the process—inside looking out instead of outside looking in.

Additionally, you need to have employees develop their own *individual* mid-term plan, and discuss it with them in depth. The idea behind this is to get the team members to think about their individual mid-term plans so they can make intelligent decisions about their long-term futures as well. I guarantee that if you practice short- and mid-term thinking, you'll have increased respect from your team and from those to whom they report.

As Benjamin Franklin once said:

"I have always thought that one man [or woman] of tolerable abilities may work great changes, and accomplish great affairs among mankind, if he [or she] first forms a good plan, and, cutting off all amusements or other employments that would divert his [or her] attention, makes the execution of that same plan his [or her] sole study and business."

LONG-TERM PLANNING

Now, let's move to the great unexplored territory: that of long-term thinking. In my book *Jumpstart Your Motivation,* I told a story about a businessman in Asia who was being interviewed by a reporter. The reporter asked the businessman about his one-year plan, his five-year plan, and then his 10-year plan. But he was most impressed by what he heard as he got up to leave the room. The businessman stopped him and said, "As for long-term thinking, I am surprised you have not taken the time to ask me about my 100-year plan." The reporter was stunned and asked the executive whether he was joking. The man replied, "No, I'm quite serious. I do have a 100-year plan for my business." The reporter responded, "With all due respect, you're 65 years old—you will not be around to execute this plan." "Yes," agreed the executive, "but my company will."

I remember the turmoil that engulfed the Walt Disney Company when Walt Disney passed away. The executives who took over the company struggled, scratching their heads and asking the question, "What would Walt do?" Apparently, Disney had not left a long-term plan in place, either in writing or verbally, for the company. The plan was in his head and died with him. The company struggled along for several years, until Michael Eisner came in and spoke those prophetic words, "Let's forget about what Walt would do. We need talk about what to do in order to move this company forward." The results were spectacular, because a new leader was now taking the company in a new direction.

I define long-term planning as planning that incorporates a time frame of 5 to 10 years. When I ask executives how many of them have a 5- to 10-year plan for their companies, for their teams, or for themselves, in 99 percent of cases I find that the answer to the question is a clear no. If you're going to effectively lead a team or organization, you need to be 30,000 feet up looking at the horizon, and you need to determine where the journey is taking you and the team. I believe that people want to be led and are tired of directionless leaders who don't have a clue. Ideally, it is better to have a 10-year plan than a 5-year plan, but let me warn you in advance: This part of planning is hard, backbreaking, mind-numbing work. On the other hand, I can tell you that this leads to remarkable decision-making and remarkable morale. The question you really need to ask yourself and the team is, "Where do we want to be in 10 years?" You should analyze every single category outlined at the beginning of this chapter and ask yourself, then the team, *as measured by specific metrics, where you want to be.* This is a true leadership question—it takes guts and courage to ask, and even more guts and courage to answer.

Additionally, take the time and energy to sit down with all your team members individually to help them develop *their individual* long-term plan for their career. Where do they want to be in 5 to 10 years? I guarantee that this will separate you from every other leader they have ever had because you will be the first to ask that question. Ever.

This book is called *Jumpstart Your Leadership*, and long-term thinking really is the spark for success. If you have a long-term plan, it will be the solid base on which to build the rest of your organization and leadership skills.

Here are five potential liability areas to watch for when doing long-term planning:

Clear the Cynics from the Room

If you're having team meetings, make sure that the cynics are not part of the process. I have seen many a meeting for long-term planning in which cynics have sat on the sidelines or at the main table saying things like "that will never work" or "we've never done that before" or "that really is a crazy idea." If you want to see the positive energy quickly sucked from the room, allow the cynic to have a voice. If you have cynics on your team, then you need to coach them in advance about what you expect from them in terms of positive behavior.

Don't Let the Past Own the Future

When looking at the future, you certainly want to be aware of the past. But you don't want the past to own the future. What does that mean? Well, let's take a look at Steve Jobs at Apple. Imagine Jobs and his group brainstorming the future of Apple, when someone first brings up the idea of a portable music-playing device. Someone could certainly say, "Well, we don't make those, because we're a computer company," or "We aren't Sony or JVC." That would be an example of the past owning the future.

Think Big

One of the characteristics that I see in leaders (which is somewhat disturbing) is that they do not think big enough. Their expectations of the future are too low and they allow people to limit their thinking. When the leader's thinking is limited, the team's thinking will be limited as well. Great leaders push organizations to reach their highest potential and get team members to think differently about the organization and the team.

Be Creative

Allow yourself to think creatively about the future and its unlimited potential. What are some possibilities? What are some wild, crazy ideas? What would happen if we tore it up and started all over again?

Play to Your Strengths

When you're looking at 5- to 10-year plans, make sure that your plan plays to your strengths and limits your liabilities. This will allow you to take advantage of and leverage the future. It will also allow you and your team to grow.

These are some things to consider as you engage in short-, mid-, and long-term thinking. Here's a question I get asked very often: "Why should I spend so much time thinking when it is entirely possible that the plans will change?" Well, the answer is quite simple. As a leader, it is much better to have a plan than not to have a plan. Yes, plans can change in today's fast-paced world. We may have to change them. However, I find that the leaders who have the greatest strength of conviction and leadership ability are the ones who have a solid vision of the future in the short-term, mid-term, and long-term. Lastly, you will certainly be much more successful if you have a clue!

I think Napoleon Hill, author of the book *Think and Grow Rich*, says it best:

> "Every well-built house started in the form of a definite purpose plus a definite plan in the nature of a set of blueprints."

WORK IT

Do you have a professional and personal short-term plan?

_____

_____

_____

_____

_____

_____

Do you have a professional and personal mid-term plan?

_____

_____

_____

_____

Do you have a professional and personal long-term plan?

_____

_____

_____

_____

_____

Have you had a discussion with all your team members about their plans?

_____

_____

_____

_____

_____

_____

_____

Write down what you need to do in this area. Now create an action plan.

_____

_____

_____

_____

_____

_____

_____

_____

CHAPTER 3

JOLT #3:
HIRE PEOPLE SMARTER
THAN YOU

"When you hire people that are smarter than
you are, you prove you are smarter
than they are."

—R. H. GRANT

GUESS what? Hiring people smarter than you are is actually smart. Huh? I find that in most organizations, managers are *specialists* and leaders are *generalists*. Let me give you a hospital example. I am sure that the chief of surgery is not necessarily the best surgeon in the hospital, or the best specialist. However, the chief of surgery should be the best leader. By the same token, I'm sure that Richard Branson of Virgin has never actually manufactured records, flown a plane as a pilot, or assembled a cell phone, but he has led a great organization for years. What we have to realize is that the work is not done by the leader; the work is done by the team. Therefore, if we hire the best team, we get the best results.

One obstacle leaders need to overcome is their own sense of ego, or in some cases, even arrogance. I have met leaders who suffer from "egotis giantitus" (a disease of the mind). This prevents them from thinking about the possibility of hiring someone who is smarter than they are in their specific area of expertise. If you're hiring someone for finance, you may not be the ultimate expert in finance yourself. So, the goal is to find the best of the best in the world of finance. Also, think about the fact that when leaders are surrounded by teams of incredibly knowledgeable people (who are smarter than they are), then the leader looks more intelligent by reflection.

TIPS FOR HIRING SMARTER

Here are nine tips to help ensure that you hire and keep the smartest and best:

Make It Your Goal to Find the Best

I see leaders in many industries who settle for a candidate who seems OK, but is not the best of the best. If you do that, you'll pay for it later. Be the tortoise, not the hare. Take your time, be patient, and make sure that you're hiring the cream of the crop.

Always Be Looking for New Talent

When you attend industry conferences and meetings, and as you network, stay on the lookout for new talent. Sometimes when we least expect it, we come across the talent we will someday want to be part of our team. Talk to these people and get to know them professionally. Perhaps even ask them to send you a resume, and put it in your file of future talent. Keep in touch with these talented individuals on a regular basis, and when you are ready to make a move, you'll have a very strong "best of the best" candidate.

Become an Interviewing Artist

Really strive to become a master interviewer. This is a skill and a science. Identify people in your organization who are known as great interviewers. Ask them whether you could sit in on one of their interviews. Be the proverbial "fly on the wall" and observe their techniques and approaches. I learned all my best interviewing skills from a gentleman named Filemon Lopez, an executive I once reported to. He taught me the subtleties of effective interviewing approaches and techniques. If internal training on effective interviewing is available, take advantage of it. Secondly, read books and take online courses on effective interviewing—you will find yourself learning a lot.

Have Multiple Interviews with Multiple People

I have found that interviews that incorporate multiple people are much more effective. So is inviting the candidate back for several interviews. Why does this work so well? Each time the candidates come back for an interview, they become more relaxed and comfortable. This allows you, as the leader, to get beyond the techniques that they've learned in their interviewing books and classes, and to try to get to the real person. Additionally, if multiple people are interviewing the candidates, one person may identify strengths or weaknesses missed by another. The reason for this is simple: some people have chemistry with one interviewer and not with another. I once had a very strong candidate who I interviewed two times; I was practically ready to make a job offer. That is when it got very interesting! I took the candidate to lunch for a third interview, and over lunch she revealed some ethical problems she had had in her last job (plagiarism), which clearly told me that she was not appropriate for our team. I believe that this problem would not have surfaced if we had only done two interviews, and if she had not been interviewed by multiple people. By the way, you'll notice the classic technique mentioned above—the all-important, infamous "meal" technique (which, by the way, works like a charm). If you want to find out more about the real person, get your candidate to dine with you. The candidate will disappear and a real person will emerge.

Look for Hidden Assets

I often find that in corporations and organizations, there is hidden talent just waiting to be discovered. I was once vice president of training and development for a large company. I received a resume from an internal candidate who wanted to fill the position of trainer. I called the human resources department to ask why they sent me her resume. They explained that even though this candidate worked in the accounts payable department, she had indeed designed and developed a significant amount of training material on her own to train accounts payable people around the country. "Besides," the HR person said, "you have to interview her— she has passion!" Of course, we interviewed her, and after several interviews and a live training audition, she was hired as a trainer. So we discovered a talented trainer who was buried in another department in the organization—truly a hidden asset. Take the time to look around your organization for talented people who are waiting for an opportunity to be recognized and to apply their hidden talents. Also, look within your own team. Are there people on your team who, if given proper development, could move into a new role or responsibility?

Hire for Diversity

I find that the great leaders hiring people are always looking for diversity. Yes, I know it's the right thing to do; it adds greatly to the company's PR reputation. The fact that leaders are sensitive to and addressing diversity issues in terms of hiring has great value. But I think there's a *more important* reason, the real reason, why you should hire for diversity. You should hire for diversity in order to get to people who *think differently.* My definition of hiring for diversity means that you get people on your team who are completely different from you. You get diversity in race, creed, color, geography, lifestyle, age and culture. The advantage of having this kind of diversity on your team is that each person brings a unique perspective to both the projects and the work. That way, you get a much broader range of opinions. So hire people who are completely different from you—in fact, the opposite of your own image. Hire people radically different from you.

Don't Hire in Your Own Image

This sounds like a repeat of the later, but it certainly is not. What I'm talking about here is hiring people who have your same personality style, or very similar ways of thinking. For example, I've noticed that leaders who are extroverts often hire other extroverts. Leaders tend to hire people who match their own style. Make sure that your team does not reflect your image and reflects a wide variety of styles.

HOW TO GET THE BEST FROM YOUR SMART TEAM

Once you have hired a team that is smarter than you, you need to treat it as such. I believe that teams rise to the challenge of high expectations, so you need to set the bar *very high*. Here are seven tips for making sure that you get to the maximum productivity and results from your smart team now.

Give Them the Objective

When you assign a project to your smart team members, make sure that they know what final outcome is expected. However, don't tell them how to do the project, just tell them what you want in terms of the final outcome. If you have hired people who are truly smarter than you, then they will probably find a better, smarter, and faster way to achieve the goal. Yes, it's hard to believe, but they will probably achieve it faster and better than you ever could. That's why you hired them to begin with! Intelligent people appreciate being given room to do the job, but not necessarily being told how. This means that we provide resources and suggestions, but then stand out of the way and let them do what they do best. I once assumed the role of director of training in an organization that had not had this position before. When the leader hired me, he basically outlined the objectives for me, stood out of the way, and said, "Go ahead and get it done—you're the expert." Not only did this make me feel confident and competent, it also allowed my manager to do his real job, which was leading a large team of people.

Give Them Lots of Leash

When you hire smart people, you need to give them lots of autonomy and a wide range of authority to get things done their way. I've seen leaders hire experts, put them on their team, and then micromanage them. This is never a good idea. Strong, energetic, and smart people do not want to be micromanaged. In fact, they don't even want to be *managed*—they want to be *led*.

Make Them Responsible and Accountable

When smart team members are assigned a project, make sure that they own their project lock, stock, and barrel. What this means is that the project is actually their responsibility. This means that they're responsible for planning the project, communicating with you about its progress, and keeping in touch with you about any developments you need to be aware of. When you give people total and full responsibility for an important project, it bolsters their self-esteem and makes them feel that they're making valuable contributions. I remember once being assigned to manage a very large project—the results of which would be presented at a national meeting. My manager and I met, he told me what his basic expectations were, and then he let me "do my thing." The results were very effective because I was allowed to apply my strengths, and because the leader went out of his way to allow me to apply them.

Don't Ever Break the Chain

I've seen the adoption of an "open-door policy" in many organizations. While I think that the policy is a positive development and transparency in a corporation is good, I do not necessarily think that it is always healthy. When I talk about breaking the chain, I mean times when employees come to you instead of to their manager or their manager's manager. I know that you don't want to discourage open and honest and free-flowing communication, but the one question you should ask is, "Have you spoken with your manager about this?" If they have not, then find out why. Is it a problem with the manager? Is it another issue? Encourage them to talk to their manager before they come to you in the future. There are a couple of reasons why this is important. First, you need to have the trust of your team. Second, if people are always running to your office to talk about people above them, then their managers will feel as if you're not respecting their level of authority. That is never a good thing.

Compliment First, Coach Second, and Reprimand Third

I find that many managers and leaders are reluctant to give compliments. I hear some interesting comments like, "Why should I compliment people for a job they're being paid to do?" and "All that is just the soft and fuzzy stuff; it doesn't really matter," and "I'm really busy; I don't have time to run around giving out softball compliments." The compliment is *absolutely free*—on a budget line, it costs you nothing! When communicating with your team members, make sure you always start with a compliment. Then, instead of going straight to the reprimand phase, first try to coach your people to the results. You will find that people appreciate being coached and appreciate the encouragement that the coaching provides. They want to succeed. This is something rare, because many leaders never get coached at all. I believe that you should save reprimands for the occasions when team members do something they know is against policy or procedure, such as a human-resources infraction or something that is completely out of line in terms of specific expectations. I used to work in an office located in Florida. One of the office policies was that on Friday afternoons, when you were leaving, you were required to lower all your window shades. One Friday I left my office without lowering my shades (I forgot). On Monday, when I arrived at work, I had a *written memo* from my boss on my desk telling me how disappointed he was by the fact that my blinds were not in the lowered position, after I had been asked twice to adhere to the policy. Yes, this is a true story. I was offended and amazed that I would be written up for such a petty infraction when it was simply an accident due to being very busy and working on 9,000 projects at once. I just plain forgot. In this case, it would have been much more productive if my boss had coached me rather than reprimanding me. So, think about the positive impact coaching can have, as opposed to the negative impact of unnecessary and often damaging (and petty) reprimanding.

Admire Their Competitive Fire

You'll often have people on your team who are very energetic, spirited, and highly competitive, perhaps even difficult—people who may be considered "high maintenance." You have to remember that these kinds of people are often the key that winds the company clock. What does that mean? The people who have competitive fire simply drive energy and enthusiasm and a certain spirit throughout a company and that is exactly what we want. Are these folks easy to manage? Nope. Pretty easy to lead? Not always. However, you'll find that these folks are high achievers, have a great work ethic, and bring a certain spark and competitive spirit to the workplace that is very difficult to create artificially. So, rather than being critical of their competitive fire, harness it and leverage it to build a strong company and team.

Here is a great quote from Andrew Carnegie about competitive spirit:

"The price which society pays for the law of competition, like the price it pays for cheap comforts and luxuries, is great; but the advantages of this law are also greater still than its cost—for it is to this law that we owe our wonderful material development, which brings improved conditions in its train. But, whether the law be benign or not, we must say of it: It is here; we cannot evade it; no substitutes for it have been found; and while the law may be sometimes hard for the individual, it is best for the race, because it ensures the survival of the fittest in every department."

WORK IT

Are you a skilled interviewer?

_____
_____
_____
_____
_____

What are your strengths as an interviewer?

_____
_____
_____
_____
_____

What do you need to improve?

_____
_____
_____
_____
_____

Do you have a diverse team?

_____

_____

_____

_____

_____

_____

_____

_____

Write down what you need to do in this area. Now create an action plan.

_____

_____

_____

_____

_____

_____

_____

_____

CHAPTER 4

JOLT #4:
COMMUNICATE WITH
ALL TEAM MEMBERS

*"Skill in the art of communication is crucial
to a leader's success.
He can accomplish nothing unless he can
communicate effectively."*
—NORMAN ALLEN

THE next element of leadership is the often overlooked and underappreciated skill of communication. Many of the leaders that I meet think they are great communicators. Many are, but the reality is that some are not as gifted as they think they are. In fact, they may need a good deal of practice. What is humorous is that in many organizations, when I ask the managers for their perception of their abilities as a communicator, they rank themselves somewhere between good and great. The irony is that when I ask employees and team members about the level of communication within their organization, they often rank communication between poor and fair. They also make comments such as,

"We really don't know what's going on around here," and "No one seems to want to share the information." So, there certainly seems to be a remarkable gap between the leader's perception of the effectiveness of communication and the team's perception in many organizations.

It is up to you as the leader not to just communicate, but to communicate in a way that is effective for the team. As stated in the introduction, if it is your responsibility as a leader to get results, then it is also your responsibility to communicate in such a way that those results occur.

WHY IT MATTERS

- In most organizations, it seems as if the managers have less and less time and are more and more squeezed by their varied responsibilities. Therefore, it is critically important, when managers communicate, that they communicate as effectively as possible.

- In many businesses, I see employees who are stretched to the limit in terms of their time and their workload. If communication can be improved on the team, the team will become more productive—and, as the old saying goes, they'll "work smarter, not harder."

- It can be difficult in today's frenetic world for people to feel connected. Effective communication helps people feel more like a team, and get that sense of connectedness.

- All the research shows that effective communication leads to raised morale, increased productivity, reduced turnover, and a workplace where people feel comfortable. All these reasons obviously build a case for effective communication.

So how does a leader become more effective as a communicator? There are certain resources available that will give an objective evaluation of your skills as a leader and communicator:

You May Want to Consider
Taking Leadership Assessments

Leadership assessments (which are either written or online assessments) test your knowledge about specific subjects. The results then indicate which areas are strengths for you and which areas need improvement. As an executive coach, I often use assessments to get objective data and feedback on the specific skills of the leader I am coaching. Another form of assessment is the 360-degree feedback assessment. This assessment is used by many organizations to collect feedback from direct reports, peers, managers, and, at times, even outside vendors. To me, what is special about the 360-degree feedback assessment is that it provides specific feedback from a variety of levels within the organization about the *perception* of a particular leader's performance. It can also be an incredibly valuable tool to increase your awareness of your strengths and weaknesses as a communicator. As a word of caution, both of these tools can be used punitively rather than developmentally. That is wrong. When using both of these assessment tools, leaders need to be willing to set their egos aside and review the feedback results objectively with an eye toward improvement.

Ask Your Team

This requires some courage, but it is certainly completely appropriate to ask your team for one-on-one feedback on your strengths in terms of communication and on the areas that they think you should improve. Keep in mind that the team will only give you honest feedback if you have a level of trust and if they actually think you want to hear the truth rather than a sugar-coated answer. The key to this puzzle is letting them know that you sincerely want the feedback and that there will be no repercussions for negative feedback. More challenging is hearing the feedback without reacting in an inappropriate manner, or getting sensitive or defensive about it. This takes pure guts, but hey, that's leadership! (Nobody said it was easy.)

Ask Your Manager

Set aside some one-on-one time with the person you report to, and ask for feedback on your skills as a communicator. Explain that you want to grow and develop and that you would like feedback on what you do well and, of course, what you could improve. Keep in mind that some companies hire leaders who are not too comfortable with providing this kind of feedback. If that's the case, then you just have to accept it as part of your company culture. Some managers in some organizations go out of their way to avoid giving honest feedback, because they want to avoid conflict, or they do not feel comfortable assessing others. They also may not have the techniques and tools to provide feedback in a constructive manner.

Ask Your Family and Friends:

Select certain members of your family (the positive and constructive ones) and ask them to provide feedback on your strengths and weaknesses as a communicator. The key in this particular situation is to choose the right time and place. Don't wait until the entire family is gathered at the amusement park, and ambush your uncle in line for the roller coaster: "So tell me, what are my strengths and weaknesses as a communicator?" I guarantee that the quality of the response will be in direct proportion to the quality of the time and place selected. I also think that the selection of the family members who are positive and constructive is critically important, because you want quality feedback, not just any feedback. Follow the same process with your friends, and ask them for feedback as well.

The key in all of this is coming to the process with the right mindset and a true desire to learn. If you have that, then people will be more than willing to give you thoughtful, relevant, and useful feedback. However, if you bring to the process concern about what people are going to say and a level of defensiveness, then your lack of authenticity will encourage feedback that is neither true nor accurate.

So, at this point, you'll have a reasonable idea of your strengths and the areas you need to improve as a communicator. Here are some other things to think about as you make sure that you are communicating effectively from a leadership role:

Communicate with All the Team Members

I know this sounds completely crazy, but in many cases, I see managers and leaders who only communicate with certain people in their departments. They may only communicate with their direct reports. They may feel as if communicating with people of "lower rank" is beneath them. This is the ultimate gesture of disrespect. In an organization where I once worked, one morning a senior-level executive walked through our department. She had the opportunity to greet at least 10 people on her way to the office of the person she was meeting with. She ignored every single one of them. After her meeting, she walked out of the department and ignored everyone a second time. I had team members coming to my office the rest of the morning to ask me why it happened. One employee said to me, "I just came by to see if you could see me." When I asked what she meant, she answered, "Well, apparently we're invisible today." Now, I'm not saying that this executive should have stopped and spoken to every team member at length. A simple good morning, a hello, a smile, or a head nod would have gone a long way and would have been a gesture of respect. (Note: this particular executive was later fired because she could not get along with her peers.) I have toured offices with leaders, and pointed out an employee walking by. Shockingly, when I asked the leaders who the employee was (are you sitting down?) they told me they had *no idea*. Here, in my mind, is the $60 million question: How do employees feel when you do not communicate with them on a regular and consistent basis? I guess a more direct question is, how would *you* feel? Some cynical, old-school managers have at different times said to me, "Why should I communicate with them? It really is not my job. That's the job of their direct supervisor. The employees and team members shouldn't be so darn sensitive!" If you don't want employees to be sensitive, hire robots or droids! But for now, keep in mind that your employees are humans with hearts, minds, and feelings. So make it an objective to communicate with all the employees on your team.

Get to Know Them

Really make an effort to get to know your direct reports. What are their short-, mid-, and long-term career goals? Where do they want to be in five years? What motivates them? What doesn't motivate them? What do they do in their spare time? What do they get a kick out of at work? Why do they work? What do they want? Many times when conducting leadership development programs, I ask managers these questions about their team members. We do an exercise with a piece of paper, and they write down the names of specific employees, and insert the questions listed above. It's a shame how many leaders do not have the answers to any of the questions, and sit during this exercise looking mildly embarrassed. Now, will you get this information all at once? No. This is information that you will acquire over time. But once you know the answers to these questions, you'll have the tools to be more strategic about leading your team members, since you'll know them on a deeper level. Now, the cynical leader will ask me whether it is possible to know your employees "too well." That is a legitimate question. I do think that there is a line the leader should not cross in terms of interpersonal relationships. If, for example, an employee wants to talk about marital problems, drug addiction, or some other highly personal issue, I think it is the obligation of the leader to draw the line. Most companies have employee assistance programs (EAPs) and other resources to help employees handle their personal dilemmas. Additionally, it is not appropriate for managers and leaders to heavily socialize with team members on the weekends. At a certain point, if the manager oversteps the line between "boss" and "buddy," the employee will get confused on Monday because the rules have been blurred and the boss is no longer a friend. This does not mean that you shouldn't have a party or get-together at your home— but it's important that you invite *everyone* on the team, and keep the party or social event to a professional level. When you know your folks better and you know what makes them tick, you'll have the keys to build loyalty, raise morale, and reach a depth of relationship beyond what most leaders are able to manage.

Have One-on-Ones with Each of Your Direct Reports

The best way to establish strong and solid communication is to have regular and consistent one-on-one meetings with your direct reports. These one-on-one meetings need to be designed for you to update your team members, and for them to update you. They should also be "calendarized"—and yes, I know that's not in the dictionary. It's a made-up word that I use to emphasize the importance of getting those one-on-one meetings scheduled on the calendar on a regular basis. In most organizations, the reason that one-on-ones never happen is that they are never scheduled. I once worked for a company for two years, and at the end of the two years, my manager left the company. At his going-away party, he came over, put his arm around my shoulder, and said, "Shawn, I really wish I could have had more time to work with you." The reality is that this manager *never* worked with me, never met with me, never coached or trained me, and was, in every sense of the word, a complete failure as a manager. I succeeded despite his lack of effort. Additionally, in one-on-one meetings it is a good idea to make sure that the meeting has a specific time limit, and that you are (to use another made-up word) "agenda-ized." Having an agenda for each and every one-on-one meeting will ensure that you have effective and efficient communication. It will also ensure that you're able to cover the items that need to be covered. This eliminates the "oh, by the way, I forgot one other thing" meeting that ends up lasting longer than it should have lasted, resulting in frustration for both parties. Here is the key: It should be up to your *direct reports* to create the agenda for your one-on-one meeting, because that is their responsibility. You'll find that when you have an agenda, the meeting flows smoothly and has a beginning, a middle, and an end.

Make Sure Your Direct Reports Do This As Well

We have spent a good deal of space establishing the importance of one-on-one meetings. It is also your obligation as a leader to make sure that any team members who report to you are also having one-on-one meetings with their direct reports. So it is up to you to hold them accountable to repeat the good business practice of having individual meetings with their team members, the same way that you have meetings with them.

Have Department or Team Meetings Regularly

At some companies, I've asked groups about their team meetings, and they've looked at me as if I had 40 sets of eyes. Evidently, these groups never have team meetings, because their manager does not think meetings are necessary. This is pure communication mythology and a huge strategic error. There are very compelling reasons for having team meetings. First off, team meetings give the manager an opportunity to communicate with the team as a group on developments and changes (both current and imminent) in the business and the industry. As with one-on-one meetings, team meetings should be time-driven and should have a specific agenda. It is up to you to decide the purpose of your team meetings. These meetings could have a variety of functions, such as informing, training, updating, following up, brainstorming, reaching consensus, disseminating company news, discussing industry developments, etc. One idea is to ask your team members what *they* would like to know and what they think should be included in each department meeting. Keep in mind that regular team meetings do not have to go on for hours, and, in fact, it is critically important that they begin and end on time.

Make Sure Communication Is Two-Way

For whatever reason, some people in leadership roles think that their job is to tell, not ask, and to talk, not listen. This is one of the biggest misunderstandings about leadership. Does the captain of a ship need to lead if the vessel is in dire danger, about to crash into an iceberg? Of course. This would be the perfect time for a captain to *tell and not ask*. But I think that is obviously the notable exception. The gifted leaders I have seen are not dictators, are better communicators, and are not creating a monologue, but a dialogue. This is important for a few reasons: First, you can't think of everything yourself. I know some of you think you can, but you can't. Second, the combined brainpower of the team is always greater than the power of one. So the point is, you have to make sure that you ask lots of questions, encourage discussion, encourage dialogue, and get plenty of feedback. Third, sound decisions arise from lots of dialogue and discussion. Finally, here is perhaps an even more important point: you get better buy-in if you've at least had a discussion with different members of your team. So make sure to listen to your team members by having meaningful discussions— you'll be amazed at what you learn and the relationships that you're able to build.

Use a Regular Communication Tool

You will be giving information out one-on-one and at those team or department meetings. Still, you need to decide on an effective tool that you will use to disseminate information to all team members between meetings. This tool could be as simple as email, a newsletter, a website, the bulletin board, or a shared drive on the department computers, or even as crude as distributed voice mail. When you have a regular communication tool you use to distribute information quickly, you accomplish two things. First, you actually have employees who feel that they are in the loop, and therefore feel valued. Second, you put an end to the proverbial grapevine that exists in almost every office in the world, which will take great strides toward stopping the rumor mill from spinning. In the absence of information, employees will come up with their own answers and will begin to spread them haphazardly throughout the organization. The only solution to this problem is to provide solid, regular, and consistent information.

Watch Your Geography

I have seen many an organization struggle with communication because part of the group is located in the same office as the leader, while other members of the group are spread about geographically. This becomes problematic because leaders communicate information to those who are local, but don't give the information to people who are in remote locations. Employees begin to feel disenfranchised and isolated—and, well, they are! So make sure to have some sort of strategy in place to keep folks in remote locations informed and engaged, or you could fall into this trap. An additional way to make sure that you do not have this problem is taking care to visit remote locations on a regular basis. Yes, today you called on the telephone and yesterday you sent an email. However, this can never replace the connection that is made when you visit a location to communicate with your team face to face.

Be Strategic about Communication Tools

I have seen many a case where leaders are frustrated because they sent an email message and it was misinterpreted, ignored, or deleted. Managers get angry when they realize that a piece of information wasn't received as they meant it to be understood. I think that every leader should decide how a specific piece of information should be strategically delivered, rather than automatically defaulting to email. When should you use email? When should you use voice mail? When should you meet one-on-one? What about meeting as a team? Each time important information needs to be delivered, you must look at each tool to determine what would be the best strategy for delivering that particular piece of information. By the way, many people I've talked to think that because information has been emailed, it has been received. The reality is that most workers across the world are completely overwhelmed by the volume of email they are receiving. Again, give thought to what would be *most effective.*

Be Direct and Honest

The greatest leaders I have ever reported to had the quality of being direct and honest without being overbearing or blunt. This is a skill that takes a while to develop but is appreciated by team members, because they always know where they stand. They also realize that no games are being played and that what is said is meant and what is meant is said. This approach does, however, take some positioning. You have to make team members aware when you hire them that they can expect open, honest, and direct communication. If you adopt a team, you need to sit down with each person individually and explain your philosophy of communication. Explain that you think being less than honest and direct is a waste of time and does everyone a disservice. That said, you also need to make sure that whenever you are direct and honest, you explain the *purpose* behind it. Since some people are not used to direct and honest communication, they may question your motive. Therefore, it is still important to explain why you are having the discussion.

Most people after a short period of adjustment actually find this kind of communication refreshing, because many times in their careers they have had managers who have been disingenuous and poor communicators. Consequently, they never really knew where they stood with that particular leader. Therefore, they could not really establish trust.

Now that we have talked about tips for effective communication, here are some danger signs to watch for:

Technology Replacing Effective Communication

In meetings, I see PowerPoint replacing effective presentations, or people making the assumption that because they sent an email they're communicating effectively. This couldn't be further from the truth. The reality is that technology should be a tool for enhancing and enriching communication, not for replacing it.

Unproductive Communication

I meet and coach executives who tell me that they have certain members on their team who consume tons of their time with two-hour phone calls. If you are talking to someone on your team for two hours, then something is definitely *wrong*. You are communicating and so is the other person; however, it's obvious to me that the communication is not effective. When this happens, try to figure out why the communication is not efficient and correct the reasons, or the root causes for the lack of effectiveness. For example, maybe those calls need to have a specific time limit, and maybe someone on the call needs to make sure that each call remains focused. I think one of a leader's greatest responsibilities is to make sure that all communication in meetings and conference calls remains focused and on task. The biggest complaint that I hear from employees is that they are often asked to participate in meetings and conference calls where they feel as if they're not getting anything accomplished. This is because the communication is poor and the time is not being used effectively. Make sure that this does not happen in your world.

Lack of Authentic Communication

I see situations in the corporate world where people are meeting and they are not saying what the real issues are, because they do not think it is politically expedient to do so. Make it clear when you hire and when you coach your team members that one of your expectations is open, honest, and authentic communication. This means that, when there is a problem, people state that there is a problem and why. Yet in many organizations, I see people talking about a topic that is not the real issue; they're just dancing around it. Unless you own a dance studio, you should not be dancing around anything. Get to the bottom of the matter and ask people for honest and open opinions and ideas. Make sure that you explain to people why open and honest communication is so critical to the success of the organization. Many times I find that people are much more willing to do anything that they are asked to do if they are given a sound, logical reason for doing so.

Disrespectful Communication

A leader should never, at any time, communicate with an employee or team member in a disrespectful or humiliating manner. There is no excuse, reason, or justification for this kind of behavior. If you want results, you must communicate with people in a respectful manner at all times. This means that in voice mail messages, email correspondence, and both group and individual meetings, it's always critical to treat people with the level of respect that they have earned and deserve. Sure, there may be times when employees do something stupid, or even something that's a deliberate act of insubordination. Your role is to always stay in the center of the storm. At one point in my career, I worked for a very large corporation and was humiliated by an executive during a meeting. She asked me why I had attended a specific conference, and when I explained, she said, and I quote, "Well, that was dumb, and sounds like it cost a lot of money. Don't ever do that again. It was a complete waste of funds, and irresponsible." I let her know that my attendance at that conference had been approved by my prior boss (who had since left the company), and she replied that she did not care. Keep in mind that this was all said in a very disrespectful tone and with a very angry facial expression in front of *13 other people in a meeting*. All the folks in the room felt bad for me and hoped that they would not be her next "victim." This is no way to treat human beings, no matter what your position, title, or level of responsibility—ever. This meeting was a very unpleasant experience for me and made me very angry about the way I was treated. So remember, as a leader, the way to get results is to have people feel good about what they do. If they feel good about what they do, they will be more productive. Am I saying that people should never be criticized for their work or get negative feedback? Of course not. What I'm saying is that there's a specific way to provide constructive criticism without humiliating employees. They'll respect you for respecting them.

FOCUS ON IMPROVING YOUR SKILLS

You might want to consider reviewing your competence in specific communication skills. Make sure that you have an in-depth understanding of specific tools and techniques for effective communication. Here are some areas that you may want to look at in order to make sure you have as good an understanding as possible of communication skills and techniques:

Listening Skills

Take one of the various assessments that are available both online and in writing to determine your level of competence in listening. We all have strengths as listeners, and areas of weakness that we need to work on. Identify your weaknesses and put together a plan to address them.

Behavioral Styles

Take a look at the field of behavioral styles. If you're not familiar with this area of psychology, then you might want to study it. Programs like the Communication Jungle, Platinum Rule, DISC, and Myers-Briggs will give you specific tools and techniques for adjusting your communication skills and style to the person you're communicating with directly. I have found that people in leadership roles who learn these techniques are then able to customize their communication approach for each team member. This can be enormously helpful and effective.

Transactional Analysis

Look at the area of transactional analysis made popular by several books back in the '60s and '70s. The most popular one was *I'm OK, You're OK*. The goal of transactional analysis is being able to review a transaction *as you're having it* in order to dramatically increase the effectiveness of the communication. You learn to identify whether someone is communicating from a specific ego state, and then you can respond appropriately to reduce conflict and enhance communication.

Body Language

Since most research shows that body language is an important aspect of communication, this is an important range of knowledge for you to grasp. Some experts claim that nonverbal communication is a much larger percentage of communication than verbal. If that is the case, then you need to be very savvy at reading people's body language so that you can understand what they're saying with both their mouth and their body.

Presentation Skills/Public Speaking

Yes, believe it or not, public speaking and presentation skills are a form of communication. I believe that leaders are often such poor presenters and speakers that their credibility is significantly damaged. I have seen many executives in front of groups at meetings. They fumble, stumble, mumble, and stammer as a replacement for words. Obviously, this is a problem. Great leaders should be able to stand in front of a room and communicate effectively and articulately so that the group gets the message and a favorable impression is made. If this is an area that you struggle with, help is certainly available. My next book, by the way, will be titled *Jumpstart Your Presentations: How to Speak Effectively with Power, Authority, and Credibility.* There are also many organizations around the world that specialize in conducting workshops and seminars to improve public-speaking abilities. Organizations such as Toastmasters, Dale Carnegie, etc. can help you learn specific speaking skills. Of course there are many books, DVDs, and other educational tools that can also help you become a more effective speaker. As a professional speaker, I will tell you this: When you get coaching and development, it helps a great deal. That said, the only way to become a great public speaker and presenter is to practice as frequently as possible. Each time you speak you get better and develop a higher comfort level with speaking. I am sure when you first learned how to drive a car you were a nervous wreck and had a fairly low skill level. Now, of course, you drive automatically, without really thinking about it, from point A to point B. The reason that you can drive effectively is that you've had an education in driving, along with feedback and coaching. Perhaps more importantly, you've driven hundreds or thousands of miles in order to build up your skill. In reality, speaking is no different. You just have to decide that you want to be good at it and put forth the effort to educate yourself and practice.

IDENTIFY YOUR WEAKNESSES

The last step to becoming better as a communicator is to sit down with a sheet of paper and make a list. On the right side of the paper, list what you need to improve as a communicator. On the left side, list your areas of strength. Then, by simply looking at your list, determine which skill you want to work on first and commit to a plan of action over the next three months. I am sure that when you do that you will increase your level of confidence as a communicator and your effectiveness as a leader in the world of business.

I think John Hallock said it best about communication:

"I've noticed two things about men [and women] who get big salaries. They are almost invariably men [or women] who, in conversation or in conference, are adaptable. They quickly get the other fellow's view. They are more eager to do this than to express their own ideas. Also, they state their own point of view convincingly."

If you want to be more successful, strengthen the foundation of communication and you will see that you'll get remarkable results. You'll also be able to work smarter as you're working harder.

WORK IT

Are you a great communicator?

_____
_____
_____
_____
_____

What are your strengths? What do you need to work on?

_____
_____
_____
_____
_____
_____

Do you use a variety of forms of communication?

_____
_____
_____
_____
_____

Do you have regular team meetings?

_____

_____

_____

_____

_____

_____

_____

Write down what you need to do in this area. Now create an action plan.

_____

_____

_____

_____

_____

_____

_____

CHAPTER 5

JOLT #5:
CREATE A MOTIVATIONAL ENVIRONMENT

"People spend a lifetime searching for happiness; looking for peace. They chase idle dreams, addictions, religions, even other people, hoping to fill the emptiness that plagues them. The irony is the only place they ever needed to search was within."

—RAMONA L. ANDERSON

I firmly and passionately believe that people want to go to work in an environment that is positive, fun, energetic, and filled with people that they enjoy working with. It is up to the leader to build this environment. This does not happen by accident, but is created—by you.

Here are some specific tips for helping to build, create, and maintain a motivational environment.

HIRE WELL

Hiring is one of the most overlooked methods for creating and preserving a motivational environment. Many people think that the environment of the workplace is the building, the desk, the computers, or the other equipment. I believe that the leader creates the environment, and that *people* are the environment. Whenever I visit an office or organization where the morale is low and there's a general lack of energy, I find the main reason is that the leader of the group has not given concentration and effort to hiring well. Your goal as a leader should be to hire world-class employees who want to work for a world-class organization. Your company is only as good as your last hire. Think about it. When your team members see personable and smart employees arriving, they make judgments about the quality of the organization. If you hire someone who is intelligent, energetic, positive, and competent, you are setting the pace for the culture and environment of the organization. If you do the opposite and hire someone who is utterly incompetent and does not fit the culture of the organization, your new team member will become a drain on the morale and energy of the group.

I once worked in a retail operation as an assistant manager. When I arrived at my particular location, I was introduced to each employee. In my first introductory meeting, I met someone I will call Mindy. (This, of course, is not her real name. I'm changing her name to protect the innocent.) From our first meeting, Mindy was disrespectful, rude, and surly. She treated employees and customers alike with a high level of distain. One day I asked the manager why Mindy was allowed to remain part of the organization. He shrugged and said, "She's been here for 19 years." In 19 years, no manager had the courage to decide that Mindy was a negative drain on the company, the team, and most importantly, the customers. Here are some tips to help you make sure that you have a procedure to follow in order to hire the best employees, who will help build and reinforce a positive motivational environment:

Have Multiple Interviews/Three-Part Interviews

See Chapter 4 for more information.

Be Selective

As mentioned earlier, the employees *are the environment*. We need to be remarkably selective about the people we choose to be future employees of our organization. Be incredibly discerning and try to eliminate the candidate in as many ways as possible. If you cannot eliminate the applicant in all the ways that you try, then most likely you'll know you have a strong candidate. Ask yourself, "Will this person not only do a great job, but also add to the energy and morale of our team?" If there's any doubt about the answer to that question, then you need to seriously reconsider making that hire.

Fire Well

At this point, you may be wondering whether you read the above title correctly. Does it really say "Fire well?" Yes, it does! I've seen leaders of organizations all over the world who have made a hiring mistake and are too afraid to fire that person or to admit that they made a mistake. It is just as bad to *keep* a hiring mistake as it is to *make* a hiring mistake. When you have determined that someone is just not working out, after you have given the employee many chances to improve, then that person simply must go. I am sure that there have been many times in your career when you were not in a leadership role that you and your teammates said things to one another like, "Why are they keeping him around?" or "Why don't they do something about this person who doesn't do her work?" or "Why do they let that person with a rotten attitude stay around for so long?" All of us have had occasions when we have quietly celebrated the departure of a difficult employee. When everyone did the "ding dong, the witch is dead" dance. Make sure that your team is not asking these questions about one of your employees. When someone isn't working out, have the guts to make the change. Do you need to be fair? Yes. Do you need to build a paper trail so that when the person is terminated there is a legal background and documentation of the lack of performance? Yes. But after all of that has been done, you need to make a move quickly to let the person go. You may want to consult your human resources department, but make sure that you pull the trigger sooner rather than later. I find that most leaders wait way too long. You have to keep in mind that that these people may already feel badly about their performance and be miserable working in a job where they're not succeeding. You could, in fact, be doing them a favor. On the day you terminate someone, make sure you meet with the person in private, are diplomatic and firm, and spare the person any humiliation or ridicule. Once the person has been released from the employ of the organization, simply ask the team to get together for a short meeting, and announce that the person is no longer with the organization. Briefly field any questions and make sure after that point that there is no further discussion or rumors and gossip about that employee. This should be nipped in the bud immediately, because it creates a negative and hostile environment, which is exactly what you're trying to avoid in the first place. Here's one other axiom that you may want to consider: one person should never be more important than the success of the team and the organization. If the organization is suffering and dysfunctional because of one person, then you have failed in your leadership role, and you need to take action. On the brighter side, being a leader means being able to take action. That action will allow you to create and maintain a positive motivational environment.

ORIENTATION

Orientation is also a misunderstood concept among many folks in leadership positions. Most people think of an orientation as a one-day event that employees attend during their first week of hire. That is not orientation. That is a class. In that class, new employees learn some information about the company, its policies, its procedures, and its benefits. As a leader, however, you should not allow this to be your employees' first and only orientation. Here are some additional thoughts and approaches for making sure that their orientation is more successful:

Orientation Should Not Start When the Person Is Hired

It should start during the interviewing process, particularly during the third interview, when expectations are laid out and we seek to get the candidate's agreement to those expectations. Orientation should also continue on the new employee's first day when the employee meets with you and receive (before the orientation class) a written job description and a review of your expectations. Both of these items should be in writing, because we know that people only hear what they want to hear. By putting everything in writing, we avoid ambiguity and confusion.

Meet and Review

Once someone has attended the orientation class, it should be up to that person's leader to sit down and review what was covered in the class. Review and reinforce key information.

Distribute the Calendar

A leader should meet with new employees and give them a specific calendar—an eight-week orientation plan. The purpose of this weekly plan is to develop and implement specific processes for employees to follow in their first eight weeks. It helps them to learn the organization and the culture. Keep in mind that when employees start they have accepted the job, but this does not necessarily mean that they have decided to stay. We need to make sure that when someone starts, the process used for orientation makes a positive impression and is packaged to convince the employee that the decision to join your organization was a solid one.

The Magic of Day One

One thing that you may want to consider is the impressions that are created by your new employee's first week. In many cases, when employees start at a company, their desk isn't ready, their computer isn't there, and sometimes it hasn't even been ordered yet. Make sure that your team gets a space ready for your new employee, so that the new person feels welcome. See that the new hire gets a tour of the entire facility, is introduced to the team, and starts to develop a good feeling about the organization. Here are some other nice touches that I have seen used to greet new team members: a card signed by the entire team welcoming the new employee aboard, a "welcome to our company" banner strung across the new employee's office, even a small vase of flowers or a box of candy. All these small gestures communicate that this is your employee's special first day.

Ambassadors

You may even want to consider finding folks within the organization that have high energy levels, lots of enthusiasm, and great personalities, and making them ambassadors. An ambassador's role is to be an integral part of a new team member's first few weeks on the job and to help with any unfamiliar situation. Ambassadors are used to make new hires feel welcome and to be their first mentor in the organization, to help them to succeed in their first few weeks.

Ultimately, new employees will have to be responsible for their own success. Still, leaders should be held accountable for making sure that they get the proper orientation— the type of orientation that leads to a positive, inspired employee.

JOB DESCRIPTIONS

I am frequently surprised by people's responses (or lack thereof) when I ask them what they do. In many cases, I find that employees don't really have a clear, well-articulated description of what they do, so they're a little confused themselves. In some organizations, the job changes every week. Due to the fact that most employees do not get a proper orientation (according to the outline above), their job descriptions are, at best, muddy. In many companies, when I ask whether there are written job descriptions, I either get people looking embarrassed or people staring at the floor and muttering, "Well, we used to," or, "We have them, but they need to be updated." I believe that *every* organization needs to have a job description for every job—in writing—which describes the specific tasks, roles, and responsibilities of the job. How does this contribute toward creating a motivational environment? Well, I believe when people have clarity about their roles, then they are less likely to be confused or frustrated, or feel undervalued. This is because someone has taken the time and energy to explain to them what their job is, both verbally and in writing. I also find that, generally speaking, people who have job descriptions tend to perform better. When they perform better, they feel better, and when they feel better, there's a more positive environment.

DON'T TOLERATE NEGATIVITY

One of the ways to ensure that you do not have a negative environment is to not tolerate negativity. Negative thinking creates negative behaviors. Let's talk about negative behaviors. I'm taken aback when this kind of behavior is tolerated in a corporation. Keep in mind that when you're in a leadership role and *tolerate* negative behavior, then negative behavior becomes the new policy. I once ordered food in a fast-food restaurant and was treated very rudely by the person who took my order. When I asked for the manager at the curbside to talk about the discourteous employee, she defended the employee's behavior and was rude to me herself. No one would want to work at that restaurant. When you observe negative behaviors, you have to correct, coach, and advise the perpetrators that their behavior is not appropriate, and, more importantly, the reasons why it is not appropriate. In many cases, I've seen people who were not deliberately being negative and did not realize the impact their behavior had on others. Another problem that I see is tolerance of negative talk. These are some of the things that I hear on a regular basis in offices around the world:

- "Well, that will never work."

- "It's a stupid idea."

- "Why would we do that?"

- "We tried that before, and it didn't work."

- "Did you hear about the_____?" (followed by a negative statement)

- "Nope."

- "Not at all."

- "No way."

- "What's the downside?"

What people don't realize is that negative self-talk leads to a negative environment and negative responses. It is almost the opposite of thinking big. Negative talk eventually leads to thinking small. It leads to minimized thinking, reduced expectations, minimized results, and cynicism. If you don't think that this is true, then simply observe a gifted coach take over a sports team that is losing. Yes, the coach certainly does make adjustments in talent. But what I find, in most cases, is that the new coach brings a new attitude and a new way of thinking—doing away with the negative talk and encouraging a positive mindset. The new coach (and often the administration) allows the team to think in a positive way, because the new coach has created—yes, a positive motivational environment.

NEGATIVE ACTIONS

You should make it clear to your team that you will not tolerate negative actions. Negative actions simply mean things like arguing, complaining, gnashing of teeth, belittling, and criticizing, along with any other negative action that is probably going to create frustration or anger. What we as leaders want to do is to try to turn the negative actions into positive actions. For example, insist that team members are no longer allowed to complain, but rather to point out obstacles to productivity and give opinions on how these problems should be solved. Complaining does nothing, but pointing out problems with solutions has an action orientation that is very positive. When you as a leader start to take these specific and tangible actions to correct negative behavior over time, you will see a change in the overall environment.

LACK OF TEAM RESPECT

One other rule that I think is critically important is to make sure everyone understands that a lack of respect for any team member cannot and will not be tolerated. (I learned this from a great leader I reported to at one time.) This means that no team members will talk in a negative way about other team members, and that everyone will treat each other with a level of respect. Now, clearly we don't have to love one another, and, quite frankly, we can't make people like one another. But what we can do is insist that they treat each other with respect and civility at work, and that this expectation is not optional. I once did an exercise during a training class in which I asked the team members to get in a circle, and each person was required to say something positive about each team member. We would start, for example, with Sue. I would then ask each team member to say one positive thing about Sue. Of course, when Sue was having compliments thrown in her general direction she was not allowed to deny them or comment on them. She was just to sit and take the positive comments. What struck me as remarkable was that many people in the circle exercise found it to be quite moving (some people had tears in their eyes), and a great boost to their self-esteem. This always tells me that team members are not giving each other enough positive feedback, and if more positive feedback were given, then people would have more mutual respect for one another.

Sure, I've had employees who said, "It's not my job to get along with everyone. My job is to come to work and do the job." My response to that train of thought is this: Being a team member is an integral part of the work, because we have to get the work done together as a team. Therefore, producing something is only half the job. The other half of the job is being a productive team member.

BE A SPARK PLUG

Now you're saying, "I have to go from leadership to being an auto mechanic?" No! What I'm saying is that it's up to you to create excitement, inspiration, and energy within your department. One of the best ways of doing this is to make sure that you walk around your department in a very casual fashion. On occasion, pop into people's offices for no reason, sit down, and have a chat to find out how they're doing. If for some reason they're discouraged or moody, it's up to you to try to help them get in a more positive mindset. That is part of being a spark plug as a leader. Make sure that you communicate on a regular basis with every team member, as we mentioned earlier, both one-on-one and in group meetings. When you're having these discussions, you'll have the opportunity to influence, inspire, energize, and coach. This is a great way to build and maintain positive morale. Make sure that you are positive yourself. If you are positive and energetic enough, you'll find in general that your people will model your behavior.

MAKE A CAREER PATH AVAILABLE FOR ALL

In some companies, I see clear career paths for the sales crew, for the executive group, or for certain specific departments. Members of departments that don't have career paths feel that they have dead-end jobs and that they'll never move up or out because there's nowhere to move to. I think this is a strategic error on the part of the leader. No one in an organization should have a dead-end job. So how do we solve this problem? Here are a few tips:

Make Sure That Every Department and Every Job in Every Department Has a Specific Career Path Available

Let's say, for example, that Joe is a shipping clerk. Sometimes people say, "A shipping clerk is all he'll ever be." The smart leader makes sure that shipping clerks (even within their specific job function) have different levels that they can rise to, dependent on their individual competence and accomplishments. For instance, the leader might create titles such as Shipping Clerk, Shipping Clerk 2, Shipping Clerk 3, Manager of Shipping, and Director of Shipping. The advantage of having that system is that it really does put an end to the dead-end job. Even if people stay in the same department for a long time, they have the ability to move into different levels based on job performance and meeting expectations.

If Possible, Promote from Within

I know that it is always a good idea to have a mix of both external and internal candidates. Sometimes it's helpful to bring fresh blood to an organization to stimulate the employees that are there. However, this being said, it's a good idea to try to promote from within, and to make the job theoretically available to all. When team members see that they have the opportunity to post for and possibly even land jobs that come up, they feel much more motivated and excited because the future has no limitations.

Make Sure Not to Pigeonhole People

On occasion in a training session someone asks me, "If I'm coaching and developing one of my team members, say a receptionist, and this person mentions a desire to be the CEO in the future, what do I say?" My answer to this question is always the same: I don't believe it should be up to us to *kill someone's dream* and to limit someone based on our narrow thinking about the person's capabilities. There are many cases when an individual in a "lower-level" position in an organization ended up eventually becoming a president or CEO. So please, do not limit your thinking, and don't allow your employees to limit theirs. As we'll talk about in another chapter, it's certainly a great idea to ask people where they want to go in their careers and to provide resources to make their dreams a possibility, depending on their effort and performance.

Seniority

I am not a fan of seniority, because I believe that it is counteractive to the creation of motivational surroundings in the workplace. It also interferes with having a competitive environment. What do I mean by competitive? I don't mean that employees are cutthroat and running over one another to achieve the next level promotion. What I am saying is that employees should at least feel as if they have the chance to move up. When positions are open and available, they should know that there's a fair and honest competition to fill the positions with the most qualified people. This is where I think seniority can be very damaging to a motivational environment. Someone who has been around for a long time is not necessarily the most qualified person for a job position or an opportunity.

HAVE FUN

Sometimes, I get an odd reaction when I advise the leaders in my leadership development programs to have fun. One of the keys to creating a motivational environment in the workplace, and creating a place where people want to go to work, is this: Make sure that you work hard, but also have fun. This contributes to employees' energy by building a high level of morale. Here are some tips that you may want to consider in order to make the workplace more enjoyable:

Plan Fun Events

Try to brainstorm events for employees with some of your senior team members. For example, I've read about some companies that have a barbecue for all their employees every other Friday during the summer months, out behind their building. This certainly adds a great deal of fun to the workplace and also creates an esprit de corps among the workers, because not only do they have a barbecue to look forward to, but they also get to meet and talk to their coworkers on a social level during a company-sponsored event. The only rule about these kinds of events is that they should always be politically and socially appropriate. This means that they should not relate to religion in any way, shape, or form. They also, of course, should be all-inclusive. Events that are not all-inclusive due to a lack of planning can eliminate certain employees from participating and are therefore exclusionary and, quite honestly, insulting. So come up with a list of events you could have during the year. Appoint someone on the team to plan and implement the details, and put the dates on the calendar in advance. You will find that it will definitely build a sense of morale and energy when employees are having fun at these events. One area in which you need to be cautious is the handling and serving of alcoholic beverages, if you choose to have them at all. I have seen many a corporate event completely ruined by a small number of employees who were completely out of control in their consumption of alcohol. Yes, those employees may be having fun because they're drunk, but meanwhile other employees are offended and uncomfortable. Plus, you put yourself in a position of liability. If alcohol is served, make sure you can limit everyone's consumption and only serve for a brief period of time. Additionally, "deputize" some key leaders in the company to monitor the consumption of alcohol and to control specific employees if they start to go overboard.

Have Celebrations

I was once involved with a sales group in which the leader of the group had the entire team set a goal. If they reached this specific goal, the entire group (and their spouses) would celebrate by going on a week-long cruise completely paid for by the company. At the end of the year, the team not only made the goal, but exceeded it by a large margin. The following spring, every employee was able to go on a seven-day cruise, all expenses paid. You can imagine the sense of team pride that was built by everyone going on a cruise together to celebrate the entire team reaching a goal. Celebrations certainly do not have to be this elaborate and expensive. Still, it's good to develop rituals and ceremonies in order to celebrate both personal events, such as someone being with the company for certain amount of time or someone retiring, and the achievement of specific business goals. Celebrations certainly do add to the level of fun and energy in the workplace and make the job more enjoyable.

Dream a Theme

Another element that you can bring into your office is to have organized "theme days" that are announced in advance. For example, you may have all team members on one specific day wear a T-shirt or jersey from their favorite sports team, and even have a sports-related lunch of hot dogs and hamburgers available for all employees over several hours. This type of approach really costs very little money but generates a sense of buzz and excitement for workers and allows them to have fun, dress differently, and break up the day-to-day routine.

Run Contests

Contests are a fun way to bring together the group, and they do not necessarily have to relate to sales or revenue. You could have a contest about increased efficiency, the number of calls made, the number of calls received, or any number of measurable metrics in which teams can compete against one another. At the end of the day, you can have a ceremony where you award the prizes, which do not have to be large or expensive. Have fun with it! Offer prizes such as a "brand new car," which is actually a miniature toy, but a car that everyone would want. (The joke must be clear to everyone from the start, of course.) Contests can be a fun way to create a good team environment where people are happy and excited and having fun by making the day different.

Gather the Team

It's a good idea as a leader to gather the team on a social basis twice a year. This might involve everyone on the team (and their families) attending a cookout at a local park on a Saturday afternoon—with the company providing the main entrees while everyone brings a covered dish. Or you could have everyone attend a baseball, soccer, or football game on a specific night, also with their families. Another approach is to buy tickets to a local amusement park and have employees attend with their families as well. Again, none of these approaches are remarkably expensive, but they do help create a motivational environment.

91

In closing this chapter, here is one final thought that you'll want to consider. Obviously, all the other concepts that are outlined in this book are applicable to creating a motivational environment. I know that if you follow every one of these principles and work on improving and installing all of them, you'll build a strong foundation for the future of your organization.

WORK IT

Do you have a motivational work environment?

_____

_____

_____

_____

_____

Do you schedule fun events and themes in the workplace?

_____

_____

_____

_____

_____

Do you have a solid orientation process for new hires?

_____

_____

_____

_____

_____

Do you have up-to-date job descriptions?

_____

_____

_____

_____

_____

Write down what you need to do in this area.

_____

_____

_____

_____

_____

_____

_____

_____

_____

CHAPTER 6

JOLT #6
REWARD EXCEPTIONAL
PERFORMERS

"The idea of thanking staff should mean giving them something that they would never buy for themselves."

—JANE COOK

I was doing a training session for one of my clients and was explaining the concept of rewarding for exceptional performances. A manager in the back of the room raised his hand and said, "I hate to be the devil's advocate, but we really have to treat every employee the same." We proceeded to have a lengthy discussion in class about the difference between meeting the requirements of human resources policies and procedures (and the law), and having the flexibility to reward employees who excel in their performance. That's what this chapter is all about. If we want to have employees who are fired up and excited, we must figure

95

out creative and innovative ways to reward for exceptional performances.

In the past, I worked for a company where I had a remarkable year in terms of performance. When I had my year-end review the company executive who was doing my review gave me exceptional numbers, in fact probably the highest that I had ever seen with that company. However, after my review was complete, the company gave me a somewhat standard increase in compensation. I was insulted by this approach. My reviewer had just told me that I was an exceptional performer, but I was getting what I considered to be a very pedestrian increase. This didn't make any sense. If you have made an exceptional performance by the company's own admission, why can't it be rewarded accordingly? I had a lengthy discussion with my manager about this remarkably confusing and frustrating concept, and his reply was, "Well, you should still feel lucky that you actually got one of the highest raises in the company. Most people this year are only getting 2 to 3 percent raises, and you got 5 percent." This did not make me feel better. In fact, the difference between 3 percent and 5 percent was so small that I found it to be highly demoralizing. I said that it was not fair in a very professional manner without getting angry, but it was obvious that the subject was not open for discussion. Ironically, the next year my review noted specifically that I had had an "inappropriate" response to my previous review. I swear to you that this is true; I can't make this stuff up. It is the source of comic strips and the greatest television comedies.

I believe that you can create a situation in which exceptional performance is rewarded. So what can you do as a leader to create a reward structure? Yes, there are laws that you have to follow in each state and country, but the innovative and creative manager finds ways to reward exceptional performance. Let's face it, in most corporate situations, exceptional performers have a healthy ego and a great deal of pride in the quality of the work that they do. Our goal, then, should be to create a systemized approach to appeal to the mindsets of the superstar performers, so that they continue to have high morale, high productivity, and good performance. How do you do that? Here are 10 tips to help ensure that you are rewarding your best so that they remain the productive backbone of your organization:

Treat Everyone Differently

It is important for each employee to have an Individual Development Plan. When you know your employees well, when you know what motivates them, when you know what spins their wheels, then you have the ability to customize your approach to each employee. Let's say you know that one of your employees' key motivators is time off. Let's also assume that there is a week the employee works lots of hours, works hard, and has exceptional results. Imagine what would happen if you walked into that employee's office on Friday afternoon at two o'clock and said, "Thank you for all your hard work this week. As a reward, I would like you to go home early today." Obviously, this would have a positive impact on the employee. First, there would be the great sense of accomplishment that comes with being in the car on a Friday afternoon, leaving work early. Then the employee would get to explain the reward to surprised family members at home. The secret to this approach is knowing what motivates each employee. Some employees would not be excited about going home early. In fact, it would irritate them. We have to figure out which approach works for each employee to customize the approach. I once worked very hard putting together a national sales meeting, which was very successful. At the beginning of the following week, my manager had a box of flash-frozen filet mignon steaks shipped to my house. My wife called from home and said, "Honey, a box just arrived, and we have wonderful filet mignon steaks waiting for you for dinner when you get home." That night I felt rewarded for my hard work, but also felt that my family was being rewarded for my absence and for their hard work as well. So think about which you can do to *customize* the reward for each employee.

Have a Reward Plan

When I talk to people in leadership roles and ask them whether they have a reward plan, they usually ask, "What do you mean by a reward plan?" My response to that question is, "What elements are you putting into place this year in terms of budget and thought as to how you're going to reward your individual employees over, above, and beyond their annual raise in compensation?" The answer, of course, in 99 percent of the cases, is that the leaders have never even given it a thought. I recommend that at the beginning of each year as part of your planning process you develop a short-term, mid-term, and long-term plan for individually rewarding employees. Obviously, this has to go into the budget. If you're going to hand out movie passes to an employee, those movie passes have to be paid out of some budget line. So think about what you can do to reward your team members for exceptional performances, and put a plan in place.

Be Creative

Try to figure out how you can be creative when it comes to rewards. Here is a list of creative rewards you might want to consider:

- magazine subscriptions

- movie or theater tickets

- bonus time off

- money in cash

- small gifts

- concert tickets

- a company car

- increased privileges
  (e.g., a better parking space)

- lunch with the boss

- an afternoon boat cruise

- gift certificates

- a shopping spree at the mall

- entry into a random drawing for prizes

- employee of the month

- employee of the year

- team of the year

You get the idea. You're only limited by your creativity, and as you can see from the list above, the rewards don't necessarily have to be expensive; they just have to be unique. Use the element of surprise, because often the element of surprise sweetens and heightens the experience of being rewarded for an exceptional performance. If you are rewarded for an exceptional performance when you least expect it, it makes the reward even more appreciated. When a reward becomes expected, that's when it can lose its excitement and impact.

Think of Categories

When you think about rewarding for exceptional performances, try to think of categories for the performance itself. You can reward for an individual performance, for a group performance, for meeting specific group goals within the team, or for a team performance. Each of these categories can have an impact on the individual and the group.

Don't Reward for a Mediocre Performance

I have seen leaders who have gotten used to rewarding for exceptional performances. When a project is done and the results are just OK, employees are still rewarded as if the results had been exceptional. This is a huge strategic error. You must only reward for a performance when it is truly exceptional—not normal, average, or standard. Keep in mind that there are mechanisms in place for rewarding standard work. What we're talking about in this chapter is rewarding for exceptional performances, which should mean just that: exceptional. So when you consider rewarding for an outstanding performance, stop to think about whether it is truly exceptional. If you are in doubt, it is probably not.

Communicate the Reward

One of the key strategic errors that I see leaders making when it comes to rewarding for exceptional performances is not communicating clearly enough *that it is a reward*. For example, if an employee does an extraordinary job on a project, a leader will go up to the person, pat the person on the back, say "good job," and hand the employee a gift certificate. This is an OK approach, but it does not exactly stress how much the leader appreciates the employee's extraordinary job. I highly recommend that the leader meet with the person one-on-one, even if it's for only a few minutes. At that meeting you should say to the employee something like, "Bill, I really appreciate your work on the project. It was top-notch and way beyond what I expected. I want to thank you for that, so please accept this certificate to LeTop Dome Restaurant as a small token of my appreciation. I hope that this weekend you and your wife can go and have a nice dinner and celebrate the fact that you did so well on this project." Do you see how this is different from the first scenario? One was just a casual mention of the reason for the gift, and the other positioned it in such a way to highlight and reinforce the exceptional performance. Ironically, I have spoken with employees who got rewarded but did not actually understand it was reward because it was never articulated as such. They thought that all the other employees got the same thing. Ouch. So if a reward is special, make it special by pointing it out and articulating the unique element of the reward.

Think Small

Leaders often say that they don't have the budget or the expense line to pay for elaborate gifts to give their team as rewards. This is an error in their way of thinking, because rewarding for exceptional performance does *not necessarily* have to cost a lot of money. For example, when I was in a leadership position, I would often write small note cards to employees thanking them when they did outstanding work.

These cards had my name embossed on the top and were handwritten and signed by me. Believe it or not, these handwritten cards seemed to have a high perceived value, because I found them proudly displayed in cubicles or on the wall as long as two years later. A well-placed voice mail made after hours can also have significant impact. Imagine an employee who comes into work in the morning and notices the phone display is showing a voice mail message. The employee reaches over, presses the button, and hears the manager say, "Well, good morning, José! This is Fred, and it's 12 o'clock at night, and I'm on the road right now in another city. I just wanted to take the time to call and leave a message on your voice mail now to let you know how proud I am of the presentation that you did yesterday." Here's the question: how much did that voice mail cost? Almost nothing, except the cost of a call. The motivational value of the call, however, is priceless. Another option that's often overlooked (as silly as it sounds) is the simple use of a compliment. I don't think leaders understand the power of compliments, and they don't use them often enough. Plus, they're free.

Don't Wait until the Annual Review

Many times, employees perform at an extraordinary level all year. However, they are not rewarded or given any kind of feedback. They aren't told how well they're doing until the ever-loving, world-famous annual performance review. Let me be blunt: this is a ridiculous way to do business. To think that in today's age of immediacy, in the fast-paced world we live in, an employee should have to wait *12 months* (or longer) to get productive feedback is absurd. When employees are performing especially well, don't just write it on a sheet of paper and drop it into their annual review file! Make a point to bring it up, making a note of it and rewarding the team member at that time. This does two things. First, it keeps the motivational fires lit because people feel that they're being acknowledged. Second, if you have a sense of immediacy and respond quickly, employees will actually be more likely to remember what they did and repeat the behavior. I've seen employees who, during a review, don't even *remember* a specific accomplishment that their leader brings up, because it has taken so long for the feedback to come. The bottom line is this: acknowledge exceptional performance sooner rather than later.

Stand on Ceremony

If there are specific rewards that you give on a regular basis for exceptional performances, make sure that you arrange an appropriate time and place for the award. I was attending one of my clients' annual dinners and was quite touched by the awards that were given out that evening. I was not touched by the awards themselves, but was amazed at how they were announced, the setup of the room, the speeches that were made by the leaders giving the awards, and the response of the awardees. It may sound ridiculous, but it almost felt like a small version of the Academy Awards or the Grammys. The leadership of the company created a special environment on a special evening where the awards were not only given, but the awardees were honored by the way they were presented. You don't necessarily have to rent a hotel room and fly people in from all over the country, but you could have a breakfast, lunch, or dinner in order to give out certain awards where people are acknowledged publicly for their exceptional performances. Here's another analogy. Imagine you're watching the Olympic Games on television, and when athletes win a medal, it's tossed to them on their victory lap, and then they run off to the locker room. It obviously would *not* have the same impact. So try to think about how you can create a ceremony in order to enhance and bring more significance to rewards.

Instill Pride

One company that I used to work for had what it called the President's Club award. The President's Club award was given each year to people who showed outstanding sales performance around the nation, and only a limited number of people received this award. The people who received it were given a fancy sports coat with a logo (like the Masters golf tournament coat), and the President's Club emblem appeared on their business cards from that point on. Every year at the national meeting, there was a gala President's Club dinner that was—of course—only for people who had won the President's Club award. This was a way of developing pride in the award and instilling it throughout the organization. Try to figure out how to set up your awards in such a way that they become a source of pride within your corporate culture and, in essence, become a badge of honor. One other great example of an effective award, that you'll often see in retail stores and restaurants, is the "employee of the month" award. The recipient has a picture taken, and the picture is proudly posted with the employee's name in a very public place.

So these are the elements you definitely need to consider when it comes to rewarding for exceptional performances. I can tell you that all the research shows that employees do not leave companies, *they leave managers.* I believe that one of the key reasons employees leave managers is that they feel underappreciated and under-acknowledged, and overall they don't feel that their efforts are noticed. This is somewhat ironic, because usually, once superstars decide to leave companies, executives scramble around, making counteroffers in order to get them to stay. I personally would rather do the work in advance to satisfy exceptional performers, so that I will not have to run around trying to keep the employees from leaving. In essence, it's almost like planting a crop. When you concentrate on rewarding exceptional performances, you're planting the seeds of satisfaction and the seeds of retention, and you're building a high level of morale among the team.

Some people will read this chapter and say, "If I treat one team member differently from the others, then the other team members will complain." This is where the art of rewarding exceptional performance comes into play. If the leader is truly connected and working with each of his team members and understands what motivates each one of them individually, then no one will feel slighted or ignored.

WORK IT

Based on what you just read, do you reward for exceptional performances?

_____

_____

_____

_____

_____

Are you creative in the kinds of rewards you give?

_____

_____

_____

_____

Do you treat everyone the same?

_____

_____

_____

_____

Do you compliment people for a job well done?

_____

_____

_____

_____

_____

Write down what you need to do in this area. Now create an action plan.

_____

_____

_____

_____

_____

_____

CHAPTER 7

JOLT #7:
HOLD PEOPLE ACCOUNTABLE
FOR THEIR WORK

"Accountability breeds response-ability."
—Stephen R. Covey

IN many organizations, I see leaders who are not willing to hold people accountable for their work. This is because either they don't know how to hold people accountable, are concerned about being too demanding, or are afraid of conflict. One of the key elements of effective leadership is that we *must* hold team members accountable for their work. I mean this in four distinct ways. First, we must make sure that people do the tasks and projects that they're responsible for. Second, we must make sure that we hold people accountable for the quality of their work. Third, we must hold teams accountable. And fourth, we must hold people accountable for their behaviors in the workplace. To summarize, we are addressing accountability for work, quality of work, and behavior.

How do we define accountability? The way that I define accountability is *roles, goals, and objectives plus responsibility equals results*. There is no question, as we've mentioned several times in this book, that leaders are responsible for results. That's what we were hired for. That's what we do to get sales revenue and profit. So here's the question: Why don't leaders hold people responsible and accountable for their work? Here are five reasons that I have found for why managers do not hold people accountable:

Fear

Some managers don't hold their people accountable because they're afraid of the response that they might get from their folks. They are fearful of the conflict that results from the honest evaluation of a project. Sure, it's easy to give people positive feedback. Holding people accountable for their work may not always be a positive activity, but it can lead to constructive discussion. Most of the leaders that I talk to have already imagined the high level of conflict that will occur when they have this discussion. This is something that leaders need to get over. A leadership role takes courage and honesty. Conversations are not always fun, but are entirely necessary. If people in leadership roles are too fearful to have these kinds of discussions, then they should either be trained on coaching and handling conflict, or should be removed from their positions.

Avoidance

Some leaders see problems in the workplace and practice what I call simple avoidance. This is the world-famous "stick your head in the sand" ostrich approach. Some leaders think that if they avoid the problem long enough, it may either go away or take care of itself. The reality is that when problems and situations are ignored too long and performance standards slip, the situation does not get better. In fact, it gets worse.

They Don't Know How to Position It

Many times in training classes I conduct, leaders say, "Yes, I agree with you. I should hold my people accountable more often, but my problem is that I don't know how to begin the conversation." There are certainly lots of techniques for approaching an accountability discussion with an employee. These techniques are actually fairly simple. First, when having an accountability discussion, leaders need to state clearly and articulately what the problem is. They also need to make sure that they are criticizing the performance, not the person. The goal of holding employees accountable is not just to correct them, but to hold them responsible for their work and at the same time make sure they will be able to perform at a high level the next time it is expected of them.

They Didn't Set Clear Expectations in the First Place

This is fairly common. The leader sits down to review the project and to hold certain people accountable for their lack of performance. However, if the expectations for the project or task were not made clear to begin with, then the employees may have a legitimate complaint about being held accountable. It is certainly unfair to expect an employee to meet expectations that aren't clear. So it is critically important when we set the expectations that they are clear and easy to understand. We also need to verify that those expectations are indeed understood.

Lack of Caring

When the time comes to hold your employees accountable, they need to know that you care about their long-term success as a member of the team. If you've shown empathy and have been caring toward the employees in the past, and if you've properly positioned the areas of accountability, then they're much more likely to take your accountability discussion seriously. This is because they know that you care about them, and are not just being hard-nosed and difficult.

So how do you, as a leader, hold people accountable? I believe that there are four specific areas of accountability that you can address. The first area of accountability involves projects and tasks, the second area involves quality, the third area involves teamwork, and the fourth area involves workplace behavior. Here are 10 suggestions for making sure that you're effective at holding people accountable for project work:

Make Sure the Project Goal Is Clear

When you sit down to review a project or a task with an employee, make sure that the goal of the project is clear, and that the employee understands it completely. One way of ensuring that this is the case is to ask the employee to restate for you the goal of the project. I have seen projects that were complete, but there was a problem. The problem was that the project that the leader thought was being done, and the project that the employee was working on, were obviously two different projects. Uh Oh! Naturally, this leads to a high level of frustration for both parties.

Lay Out the Expectations

Once the goal of the project has been made clear, it is also important to lay out your expectations. What exactly are you expecting your team members to do as part of the project? Are you asking them to lead the project, manage it, and be responsible for all the results? Are you asking them to be part of the team? Is the entire team going to be held responsible for the results? I have generally found that it is highly effective to ask the employees to put the expectations of the project in writing and send it back to the leader to confirm understanding.

Define Who Is Responsible

I learned this technique from one of the best leaders whom I have ever reported to. When he gave me a project, he would explain that it was *my project*, which meant that I was responsible for the results and for following up with him. This clearly put the responsibility in my ballpark, not his. He would then go on to give several examples of what this would look like. He would say, "This means that if we need to schedule a meeting to discuss the project, it will be your responsibility, not mine. Also, following up on the progress of the project will be your responsibility." This explanation about who was responsible for the project, in essence, took the responsibility off his plate and put it squarely onto mine.

Specificity

I'm sure you've often read about smart goals with the SMART acronym. I am not necessarily a proponent of all the elements of SMART goals (you may know SMART goals are specific, measurable, achievable, realistic, and timely). I'm not really a fan of the A and the R in the SMART formula. Here's why: As a leader, you should not always give team members projects that are achievable, nor should you always give them projects that are realistic. Sometimes people need to stretch. I am, however, a fan of the S, M, and T parts of the SMART formula. So let's start with specificity. It is incredibly important that a project's goals, expectations, and details be as specific and clear as possible. There is no room for ambiguity, because we can't hold someone accountable for something that's ambiguous. So the more specific and clear you can make instructions regarding guidelines, the better off you are. Additionally, I have always believed that when assigning a task, you're much better off meeting face-to-face than sending an email or talking on the phone. There are multiple advantages to meeting in person in terms of more effective communication and feedback, which you would miss if the project expectations were delivered in another way.

Measurement

If you're going to hold someone accountable for project outcomes, then there must be specific measurements or metrics assigned to that particular task. For example, a leader might say to an employee, "I need you to organize the files." Obviously, the employee can organize the files, but if there are no measurements or methodology, this cannot be a project for which the employee is held accountable. If, however, the manager says, "I want to walk you through this file project," and proceeds to talk about how many files there are, how many need organization, how they should be organized, and which files they are, then there might be a reasonable case for accountability. By the way, this doesn't mean that the measurement system must always come from the leader's mind or mouth. One great question that a leader can ask an employee is, "In getting ready to work on this project, how would you suggest that the results be measured?" This will also get better buy-in, because when employees are asked for ideas about measurement, they're much more likely to buy into the final expectation.

Timeline

The last part of assigning a task or project is to make sure that there's clarity on the timeline. This means setting exactly when the project is due to be finished, and also specifying precisely what being finished means. I often see conflicting interpretations of due dates between a leader and an employee. The leader said it was due by the fifth of the month, meaning it was due by the end of the day on the fourth. The employee, however, thought the deadline was by the end of the business day on the fifth. You can see that this approach will certainly lead to conflict. I have found that one of the most effective ways to hold employees accountable for a project's timeline is asking them to create a project plan with a timeline. Yes, employees often resist this approach, and they don't necessarily like doing it. But there is a compelling reason for them to do it. When they take the time to plan the project in a calendar form, they're much more likely to be successful.

Scheduled Follow-Up

As part of the plan, your employees should also have scheduled follow-ups that are on their project's calendar. As a leader, you should hold them accountable for these follow-ups. You need to make sure that they understand that it is their responsibility to schedule a follow-up on your calendar.

Project Review

Another critically important element of holding people accountable is having a periodically scheduled project review. The project review can be a one-on-one with you and the specific employee, or you can have a meeting with the team to have members review the project with the project leader and discuss what is going well, what could be improved, and what could be changed. An additional form of project review is lovingly called the "postmortem." The postmortem is simply a project review that is done after the project is entirely complete. A postmortem can be very valuable because the review of the project is happening with the advantage of hindsight. The format for this project review is simple. Have each person write down in advance a list of what they think went well and what could be improved. This can lead to some valuable discussion that will not only create an environment of accountability, but also allow people to learn new skills and thought processes that can be applied to future projects.

Monthly Report

Ask your team to create a one- to two-page monthly report. The purpose of this report is for them to give *you* an update on the current projects and tasks they are working on, the status of each project in terms of percentage complete, and what they plan to work on the following month. This is an incredibly effective tool for keeping people accountable. If people know that at the end of each month on a specific date they're going to have to report their progress to their manager in writing, they are much more likely to be disciplined about completing specific tasks and projects. How do I know this? I once reported to a leader who insisted on a monthly report, and believe me, it made me more accountable and productive. One additional side benefit of the monthly report is that you can immediately spot projects and tasks that show up and are incomplete month after month. This will allow you to investigate why that particular project is stuck in neutral, and get the project moving in the right direction. Incidentally, we should also hold employees accountable for submitting their monthly reports in a timely fashion. If the report is due on the 30th of the month, that means that the report is due by the end of the business day on the 30th. It does not mean that it can still be submitted on the 31st or the 1st or the 2nd. If you set up a monthly report structure and allow reports to be handed in late, it completely undermines the importance and the effectiveness of the report. When you allow violations of policy, those violations become the new policy and your efforts are wasted. Additionally, after one month of reports have been filed, we should not have to remind people to submit their reports. We have (in theory) adults working for us—and it is not our job to babysit them or hold their hands through their respective tasks. This enhances your credibility as a leader and teaches your employees the importance of responsibility and responsiveness.

Communicate, Communicate, Communicate

Nothing happens if you don't communicate regularly, consistently, and clearly. The best way to ensure that you are communicating is to "calendarize" it. No, that is not really a word—but if something's not on your calendar, it just doesn't happen.

Those are 10 tips for holding people accountable for their work. The next area to address is the area of quality. There are a few problems with quality. One of the issues with quality is that many people find it hard to define. So I believe that the meaning of quality has to be clearly articulated by you, in terms of both expectations and accountability. So when assigning a task or project, it is important that you articulate a measurable level of quality. For example, let's say that you're assigning a member of your team to create a newsletter for your division. How do you define quality when it comes to the newsletter? Is it the content? Is it the appearance, the meeting of deadlines, the quality of the writing? You get the idea. If you're sitting down with a staff member to discuss the creation of a newsletter, all these areas need to be covered. One way to do this is to give people samples. Show them other newsletters that you think represent the quality of the kind of newsletter that you want them to create. Discuss the quality of the content, list what you think should be included in the newsletter, and talk about all the other measurable elements. So the first step toward quality is making sure that the standards and expectations are clear. The second step is still holding your employees accountable once the project is complete. Going back to the newsletter example, let's say that the newsletter has been published for six issues, and every issue has been over and above the expected level of quality. You should certainly give the team member feedback on how delighted you are with the consistent quality. However, let's say in month seven the newsletter suffers greatly in terms of the content and the quality of the pictures. This is what I call a "coaching moment." It's a moment when performance does not match the expected criteria. If, at that critical moment, you cannot take the opportunity to coach your employee about your standards of quality, then I guarantee that the quality will be just as poor in month eight. But if you confront the employee about quality in month seven and review your expectations, then I'll bet that the quality will dramatically improve in month eight. As leaders, we need to be constantly vigilant toward dips in quality, and we have to immediately address them when they occur. Otherwise, quality will slip and people will become apathetic. I believe that people genuinely want to take pride in their work, and want to feel that they belong to a high-quality team that produces world-class results. Let's face it; no one wants to produce schlock.

The next area of accountability is team accountability. This is definitely the area where the degree of difficulty is raised. After all, this is not you holding individual team members accountable, but you actually getting the members of the team to hold each other accountable.

The first step in team accountability is convincing the team members to hold each other accountable in the following areas: meeting deadlines, maintaining quality, being honest with one another, and treating each other with respect on a daily basis.

The next step is holding the team accountable during staff meetings. Assign the responsibility of a staff meeting to each team member on a rotating basis. This means that a specific team member is responsible for running each staff meeting and for preparing for the meeting, with your guidance. This is a great learning opportunity and takes employees who once found staff meetings boring and mandatory and makes them involved and accountable.

The last area of accountability is behavior. Every organization has a specific culture, and each company and team has behavior that is deemed appropriate and productive, and behavior that is not.

So those are some thoughts about accountability, a great leadership tool (possibly *the* leadership tool). But before we complete this chapter, there's one other element to discuss, and here it is. In a leadership role you need to take remarkable care that you are *modeling* accountability. Are you accountable to yourself? Are you accountable to your company? Are you accountable to your team? If you are not, it is going to be very difficult for you to get your team members to be accountable. Imagine you're at a doctor's appointment and your doctor is telling you that you need to stop smoking because it's dangerous to your health. But in the middle of the lecture, you notice a pack of cigarettes on the doctor's own desk. In other words, for every concept that we've discussed in this book, you have to practice and preach it on a daily basis. Otherwise, you will damage your leadership credibility.

As Jack Welch, the former chairman of GE, once said:

"The world of the '90s and beyond will belong not to managers or those who make the numbers dance, as we used to say, or those who are conversant with all the business jargon we used to sound smart. The world will belong to passionate, driven leaders—people who not only have an enormous amount of energy but who can energize those whom they lead."

WORK IT

Do you hold people accountable?

_____

_____

_____

_____

_____

_____

What are your strengths in accountability?

_____

_____

_____

_____

_____

_____

What aspects do you need to improve?

_____

_____

_____

_____

_____

_____

Do you objectively measure performance?

_____

_____

_____

_____

_____

_____

Write down what you need to do in this area. Now create an action plan.

_____

_____

_____

_____

_____

_____

CHAPTER 8

JOLT #8:
COMMIT TO THE INDIVIDUAL DEVELOPMENT OF EVERY TEAM MEMBER

"Train everyone lavishly; you can't overspend on training."
—Tom Peters

IN this chapter, we're going to talk about the power of individual development. Why does it matter? There's no question that all the research shows that when employees get individual development, morale increases, enthusiasm rises, and employees feel validated and supported. Therefore, it is critically important as a leader to provide development for each employee. Different generations perceive work in different ways. We know that generation X and generation Y only stay at a company long enough to gain new information before moving on to the next employer. This makes individual development even more critically important as the retention tool for members of generation X and generation

Y. Lastly, individual development offers a way out of the dead-end job. Often when we go to parties, we hear friends and acquaintances talking about being in a dead-end job, with the usual complaints. The beauty of having an Individual Development Plan for each employee is that it literally takes any job and gives the person a future (with hard work, of course) that is very bright.

Here are 11 elements that you need to understand, relating to the individual development of employees:

Everyone Gets Development

Don't be arrogant, be fair. If you have a department with 16 employees, then that means that *each and every* employee deserves individual development. Yes, you must make the time and spend the energy. I remember sitting and talking to one employee about her future goals. She shyly looked down at the floor and her face turned red. When I asked her what was wrong, she looked up at me and said, "I've been working for almost 30 years, and you are the first leader I've ever reported to who has actually asked me *what I want.*" This was obviously a delightful development for her. In a recent meeting with a client, both the head of HR and the head of marketing had started as administrative assistants to the CEO. When I asked, "Is that the normal track?" they said, "Well, one of our other executives started that way as well. We like to promote from within." Think of the morale that is built when everyone, and I mean everyone, knows that this kind of advancement is a possibility. In one of the organizations that I worked for, in my Individual Development Plan meeting, I said that my goal was to be vice president of learning and development. That position, by the way, did not exist at that point. Did my manager shoot it down? No. In fact, about one year later, I was given that *exact* position.

Individual Development Should Not Be Part of the Annual Review Process

In many organizations, people in a leadership role will combine the annual performance review with an Individual Development Plan meeting. These two meetings should be held at separate times. I strongly recommend that you have a separate IDP meeting with each employee that is distinct from the annual performance review. Why? We know which part of the meeting gets shortchanged. Haven't we all seen it happen a million times? The performance review is first, and then in the short time that remains, the IDP meeting is held. It is rushed, which sends a strong signal that it's important but not really important *enough*.

Have an Individual Development Plan Meeting:

Each year you should have an IDP meeting with each employee. This meeting should last for around 60 minutes and should be an interactive dialogue between you and the employees, to determine their future career goals. You also need to discuss what each of you can do to develop them individually, in order to get them ready for promotion to roles that they want to serve in the future. At that point, the manager and employees should decide on a specific and measurable Individual Development Plan that will be rolled out over 12 months, starting immediately after the meeting. The purpose of the IDP is to help employees reach their career goals and aspirations. It should be your role as a leader to help people get where they want to go. After all, people do not work for a *company*. In reality, they work for *themselves* to better their own lives. Your goal as a leader is to be inspirational and help them raise their sights and think about their future.

It Should Be Their Responsibility

Once the IDP meeting has occurred, it should be the responsibility of the employees to make sure that the plan is rolling forward. It is their responsibility to take the actions that were decided on in the IDP, and it is up to them to schedule and set up meetings to update you on their progress. Why? Because they have to own it, not you. What is your responsibility? It is your responsibility to ensure that they're following up with you. It's also up to you to provide resources and work to help them achieve their Individual Development Plan each year.

Make Sure There Is a Timeline

As we all know, people lead very busy lives. You can have a very nice IDP meeting, but if the action items are not put into a specific timeline in a calendar, then they just will not happen. One thing that is very helpful is to ask the employee to develop a project calendar or update calendar in order to articulate the specifics of the plan.

You Have to Care

I know this sounds like an odd statement, but if you're going to help people and coach them through their IDP, then it is essential that you actually care about the results. What do I mean by that? If you are not truly committed to caring about the results, your employees will be able to tell that you're not being authentic and that you're just going through the motions. You can't fake it. One question that often comes up in my discussions with people in leadership roles is, "How do I care if I actually don't *like* the person who is reporting to me?" Well, it really is your responsibility to figure out a way, psychologically, to develop a sense of caring. If you don't like the person, you can certainly concentrate on the opportunity to make a difference in someone else's life, and as a leader you know that you get better results by developing each employee. Make no mistake, you must figure out a way to care, because if you don't care, they will know. It will come through in everything you do; you will reek of insincerity. No one respects an insincere leader.

They Have to Care

When you sit down with particular employees to create their IDP, they also have to care about growing and developing and they have to be committed to the plan. If they don't care about the results, then the meeting is simply an empty exercise. Why bother? If you sense that a specific employee does not care about the IDP, I think you need to have further in-depth discussions before moving forward. It is important to get to the bottom of the person's motivation, or lack thereof. If you cannot convince an employee that an IDP is an advantage and benefit, then it may not be advisable to do one at all. Maybe delaying or deferring the conversation a few weeks would help. There are some people who are satisfied with where they are and with what they do and have little or no interest in growth. That is OK for them, but I must say I wouldn't want them working for me. I will take a growth-oriented person any day over someone who isn't.

Don't Discount People's Dreams

It is not up to you to squash potential. "Dream killer" is not in your title, but "dream builder" should be. Your role and responsibility in a leadership position is to build people up and to help them move toward their dream. If I have a cleaning person who wants to be the CEO, it is not fair for me to say that this is not possible. So in this situation, it is up to me to do an analysis and talk to the person about the skills needed to be CEO versus the skills that the person currently possesses, and to help the person start working toward that goal. I will explain that it will take a lot of work to reach that position, but it is not up to me to say what an individual can or cannot accomplish! Besides, there are many famous cases in which people who were security guards or cleaning people have indeed eventually become the CEO of their company. For instance, the founder of Wendy's started out as a grill cook. Imagine how excited people would be if they actually had a discussion with you about becoming a vice president, and instead of laughing them out of your office, you said you would work with them on a plan to make that happen long-term.

Be Flexible

As you consider individual employee development, it's also important to embrace the concept of being flexible. There may be times when an employee decides to leave your department (perhaps for that cool job in marketing). There may be times when an employee decides to leave the company. These people may be honest and say they aspire to another career. It will be so darn frustrating, because you've spent a great deal of time and energy developing them, only to have them leave. Guess what—this is how the real world works. This is where flexibility can be an asset. Remain flexible in your thinking and in your possible approaches. I'm sorry to say it, but not everyone stays in a job—most people leave. But at least you have helped them define their path.

They May Not Know What They Want

I am an executive coach and work with high-powered executives, helping and coaching them. At least 50 to 60 percent of the executives I coach don't have an answer when I ask them what they want. They are puzzled, confused, and perplexed. That is, after all, why they need a coach. So don't be surprised if the employee that you're sitting down to talk to about an IDP says, "I don't know what I want." This is a very common response. Why? I find that many times people get caught up in their work and don't actually make time to *think* about the work they're doing, or to think long-term. It then becomes your responsibility to be a coach and a mentor, to help them decide what they want to pursue in the future. This may not happen at the first meeting. It may take some time and a couple of meetings before they settle on some path to pursue. Lastly, don't let your personal, biased ideas and opinions shape what an individual employee wants to do. You may think that your employee's idea is ridiculous and absurd, unrealistic, or just plain silly. But it is not your life, and your goal is merely to coach and direct. The entire idea is to get people motivated and fired up about what they do currently and what they want do in the future.

Mention the IDP in the Hiring Process

Make sure as you put potential employees through the interviewing and hiring process that they understand that if they're hired they will be getting an Individual Development Plan each year. This sets the stage for them to accept this approach enthusiastically once they are hired.

These are some of the elements that you need to consider in terms of the individual development of your employees. It sounds great, doesn't it? However, please keep in mind that there may also be some liabilities to individual employee development:

Jealousy

When you spend time with each employee and work out an IDP, it is entirely possible that one employee will become jealous of the time and development you're spending on another. This is actually fairly simple to deal with. When the issue arises, you simply need to speak with the jealous employee, and say to them, "As you know, I am committed to developing each person in our department. The same way that you have an IDP, so-and-so has one as well, and this is part of that process." This should solve any issue that comes up.

Keep It Private

When you have the IDP meetings with your employees, state at both the beginning and the end of the meetings that the discussions you have are confidential, and that you will keep anything that is discussed private on your part. If employees want to share what you discussed with their colleagues, that is their decision—but you will not be sharing with anyone except perhaps your boss or a representative of human resources. This is important, because confidentiality breeds trust.

Involve Human Resources

It is a good idea to arrange a time to sit down and talk to representatives of the human resources team in your organization, in order to fill them in about what you're doing. This way, they will be aware of what's going on if any issues come up.

Not a Guarantee

It is critically important, when you have IDP meetings, that you tell each employee very clearly that there are no guarantees about their future positions or promotion. This is important because you don't want employees to mistakenly assume that if they commit to the IDP, then they're guaranteed to land the position that was discussed. I know from lots of experience that people often hear what they want to hear rather than what was said. So make sure to emphasize the fact that there are no guarantees. This will save you from potential liability in the future.

The key here is to make sure to make a commitment both to the process and to the time that it takes. The biggest error that you could make is to announce the process, have the meetings, and then not follow up. That would be very damaging to both morale and productivity.

As the Chinese philosopher Lao Tsu once said,

"When the best leader's work is done the people say, 'We did it ourselves.'"

WORK IT

Does everyone on your team get an IDP?

_____

_____

_____

_____

_____

_____

Is anyone excluded? Why?

_____

_____

_____

_____

_____

_____

Are you flexible about each person's plan?

_____

_____

_____

_____

_____

Do you care about each person's outcome?

_____

_____

_____

_____

_____

_____

_____

Write down what you need to do in this area. Now create an action plan.

_____

_____

_____

_____

_____

_____

_____

_____

CHAPTER 9

JOLT #9:
TELL THE STORY
CONSISTENTLY AND REPEATEDLY

*"Man is eminently a storyteller. His search
for a purpose, a cause, an ideal, a mission
and the like is largely a search for a plot
and a pattern in the development of his
life story—a story that is basically
without meaning or pattern."*

—ERIC HOFFER

I have had the privilege over the last 23 years of working with many great and gifted leaders. What I have noticed is that the truly gifted people in leadership roles have the ability to tell the story consistently and repeatedly. In fact, great leaders throughout history have all had the ability to tell compelling stories to reach and connect with the public. Martin Luther King Jr., Nelson Mandela, Margaret Thatcher, Winston Churchill, John F. Kennedy, and Ronald Reagan were all known for being able to connect with a listening audience through the use of effective and compelling stories. What is the story? Well, the story is simply the story that leaders are able to tell about themselves and their team, their area or division, their products, and their company. When a leader is able to clearly articulate a compelling and motivating story in each of these areas, people get excited about the message. The story may be delivered in the form of a one-on-one conversation, a small-group meeting, a keynote address, a video segment, or a radio interview. No matter what, you must have a compelling story to tell. That's what great leaders do.

Let's take a close look at each of these components individually.

The Story about Yourself

Great leaders are able to tell a story about their background and history that is not an act of arrogance, but an act of inspiration and clarification. People want to know more about the person and character of their leaders. For example, when I was vice-president of learning and development for a Fortune 500 company, I developed a very comprehensive story that I told people when they asked me how I got to my position. My story was very simple, and went something like this: "I have been in training and development for over 15 years, but the way it started is fairly interesting. I was working in sales for a company as a territory sales rep. One morning, out of the blue, the phone rang and I got a call from the director of training and development at the company that I worked for. He asked me if I would be interested in becoming a trainer. I asked him why they decided to contact me, and he said that he had noticed some of the presentations that I did at regional meetings, and thought that I did a good job. I interviewed for the position, and decided to change my career from sales to training and development. Once I got into training and development, I discovered my true passion and my life's work. The act of writing, designing, and developing a training program and seeing the results that it made in people's lives was something that I found satisfying and remarkably gratifying. I have since written, created, and designed over 100 training programs on sales effectiveness and leadership. I've continued to work in training and development ever since."

By telling the story in that manner, I believe I was not only telling a story but also reinforcing my experience and credibility and making my passion for training and development known. It seemed to work fairly well, but here is what I do not want you to miss. The goal of telling the story is not just to get the story told; it is to get across messages in a way that is both compelling and entertaining. I could have given people a bullet list detailing my experience and background, but I don't think that would have been nearly as interesting for them. Plus, the content of the message would not have been as memorable. So, what is your story as a leader? I want you to work on developing a story that is compelling and also gets across the messages that you're trying to deliver to your team members. Here are some questions you'll want to ask yourself when developing your stories:

1. What values do I want the team members to get and understand?

2. What behaviors do I want the team members to get and understand?

3. What parts of my mission do I want to emphasize?

4. What parts of my vision do I want to emphasize?

5. What parts of the goals of my team and organization do I want to emphasize?

6. What specific examples can I think of that would make compelling stories and illustrate these key points?

The Story about Your Team

What story would you tell about your team when you speak to them, and what story would you tell about your team when you speak to others? As a leader, when you tell stories about your team to your team, you're really doing two things. First, you're reinforcing the positive aspects of what they do, and second, you're telling them stories that help them aspire to do what they should do in the future.

The stories that you tell about your team to others should be stories about your team's performance and achievements, but with compelling anecdotes, examples, and analogies. I recently heard an interview with the CEO of the advertising agency that created the duck mascot for the Aflac insurance company. She told a funny and interesting story about how the mascot was created. Sure, she could have come up with lots of facts and research and demographic information about why the duck appeals to a certain audience, but the reality is that the story she told was much more humorous and memorable.

The other approach that you could take to telling stories about your team is to tell the team specific stories about other teams and how those teams have been successful. I have seen many leaders use sports analogies to illustrate key points about the value of teamwork. These can be very powerful analogies and metaphors to reinforce the key point you're trying to get across. Make sure, however, that the stories you tell about other teams are not all sports-related. Why? Some people are not sports fans, and they won't get the analogies. Use a number of business-related stories you read about in the trade journals, or other stories that are historical in nature, to illustrate the points that you're trying to make.

The Story about the Area or the Division

This, much like the story about the team, is a story that's told about and to the area or division. The purpose of this story is to inspire and get commitment from each member of the group, and to make the members feel proud of being part of their team. I once worked for a very gifted leader who told some success story at almost every team meeting. He always made sure to tell us that he felt the team he had assembled was world-class, and that he had the best in the world working for him (he also believed it). This built pride and morale on the team. It's critically important when telling stories to also give people updates and news about what's going on in the division itself. One of the biggest complaints that I hear from frontline workers is that they feel as if they are out of the loop and don't really know what is going on in the company, on the team, or in the division.

The Story about the Products and Services

Leaders need to be able to tell stories about their company's products and services that are compelling and, in some way, convey the sales message. Every year Steve Jobs, the CEO of Apple, created a buzz of marketing excitement when he got up on stage to tell stories about Apple's new product. He presented products in a way that was both compelling and detailed. People loved attending that conference to see what kind of new, special product Apple had available. Keep in mind that people go to work for companies, but don't necessarily decide to stay. So part of your role is making sure to continue selling people on the value of your company's products and services. Every time Richard Branson of the Virgin Group speaks, it is pure showmanship. Brian Tracy, a noted speaker and author, once said, "Selling is a transfer of enthusiasm." I would like to take that step further. I believe that leadership is a transfer of enthusiasm, and as a leader you should be able to transfer your enthusiasm from you to your team. The way to do that is through stories. In one Fortune 100 company that I worked for, the CFO was famous for telling a story about money. He told how 15 years earlier he and the CEO and founder of the company had checked into a hotel when traveling on the road. It was one o'clock in the morning and both of them were exhausted from traveling for weeks. In spite of this, the CEO took the time to ask the hotel for a discount on the rooms. He received the discount by asking for it, and the discount was 20 percent. The CFO then proceeded to take the group through the difference between the cost of the room and the paid price. He explained how that money, invested in company stock over a 15-year period, represented over $500,000. This was not really a story about dollars; it was a story about the importance of being thrifty and controlling company expenses. Yes, the CFO could have said, "OK people, let's all be thrifty with our money," but you can see how the story was much more interesting. In fact, it got to the point that at company meetings the CFO would get requests for the "hotel story."

A story is a way to transform facts and figures from data to entertainment, so that at some point, stories are actually requested. You need to develop some stories about your company's services and products that reinforce the company's core culture.

As you know from reading this book, I am a professional speaker. If I am speaking to a potential client about doing a keynote address at a meeting, we talk about logistics, details, and pricing structures. To me, what is more compelling is to talk about the reactions that I often get from members of the audience when I do my keynote on the 10 Foundations of Leadership. I tell a story about a man who came over to me after my keynote, shook my hand with tears in his eyes, and said, "I have taken many courses in leadership, but today I finally realized the impact that my leadership can have on my team. I really never realized how big of a legacy I can have."

The Story about the Company

As a leader, it is your job to be an ambassador, and—I know it's shocking—also an evangelist for your company. One of the most compelling ways to do that is to tell stories about the company and its history, culture, and values. In Chapter 2 we covered the importance of having a mission and vision statement. So work on figuring out what stories you want to tell about the company, stories that you feel would reinforce the value of the company and build company pride and ownership in each individual employee.

Anyone notice the title of this chapter? It is "Tell the Story Consistently and Repeatedly." The reason I say this is that I've noticed by observation that all effective people in leadership roles tell the story repeatedly, and they tell it consistently. The CFO I mentioned earlier told the hotel story the same way every single time. He told it hundreds of times, to groups of front-line employees and to groups of executives, and every time, the story was the same. Why is it important to tell the stories repeatedly? All of us know that you never actually get all the details of the story on the first go-round. Our goal as leaders is to make sure that we set up and reinforce those messages, and repeat them on a consistent basis so that they literally become part of the fabric of the team's and the company's daily operation. It may sound a little bit like brainwashing, but the ultimate goal is that when other people in your team talk to prospective employees, vendors, and suppliers, the stories they tell will be eerily similar to ones they have heard told over and over and over. This is one of the key ways that culture is built—stories are first told around the campfire by the original storytellers, and eventually get taken up by listeners who have learned them so well that they can tell them themselves.

AREAS TO WATCH OUT FOR WHEN TELLING STORIES

Here are some key areas to watch out for as you seek to become effective and compelling when telling stories in a leadership role.

Check Your Ego at The Door

People already know you're the leader—the senior vice president, the CFO, or whatever position you happen to hold. You already have positional power, so you don't really need to flex your positional muscles when you speak to a group and tell the stories. I see many leaders who speak to groups composed of people in high-level positions. What audiences find the most charming is a person in a high-level leadership role who is down to earth, compelling, and—most of all—authentic. A somewhat humble attitude is refreshing. The other reason why this is important is that you want to have people on your team who do not possess an egomaniac persona, because that will certainly be a turnoff to both clients and vendors. Your goal is to model appropriate behavior so that your people can follow your lead.

Be Prepared

When you are telling your compelling story about all the topics we have discussed, make sure that you are fully and completely prepared. I can tell you that many times I have attended clients' meetings where a person in a leadership role was remarkably unprepared, clumsy, lacking in charisma, and incredibly boring. I think that the main reason for that kind of presentation is lack of preparation. Unless you're a remarkably gifted speaker or presenter, it is very difficult to give a presentation or a talk just flying by the seat of your pants. Depending on your level of responsibility in the organization, the opportunity to speak publicly may only occur one or two times per year. It is your responsibility to put forth the best effort possible, because that is what you owe your listeners.

Don't Make It Too Long

Whatever presentations you are giving, try to make them brief and compelling. I once attended an annual banquet at my community's Chamber of Commerce, which I had looked forward to greatly, because the governor of our state was giving the keynote speech. Unfortunately, the governor got behind in his schedule that day and arrived at the dinner meeting over 45 minutes late. Most of us in the audience assumed that because he was running so far behind schedule, he would shorten the length of his comments. Unfortunately, due to his large ego or lack of a plan B, he still insisted on giving a 45-minute presentation. The audience was made up of about a thousand people. It was a weeknight, and many had left children at home with babysitters and other caretakers. I heard people commenting that they were shocked that the governor took so much of their precious time by not keeping his comments brief. You're always better off leaving people wanting more than wanting less.

Try to Make It Interactive

If you're meeting with any group to tell stories and present, try to figure out as many ways as possible to make your presentation interactive. For example, you may decide to give a brief 10-minute presentation including some stories and facts, then open up the floor to questions. A Q&A

session is always good, because it makes a presentation immediately interactive and allows the highest connection with you as members of the audience both ask and receive answers to their questions. If possible, it is also a good idea to remain after the formal meeting has ended to chat with people informally and see whether they have any other thoughts or comments about what you said.

Give Credit in Your Stories to Others

When you tell stories, particularly about successes and victories, make sure to give credit to others. As you know, people like getting credit for their hard work and efforts. It also develops a sense of pride and team morale when team members hear you telling stories and the star of the story is not *you*, but *them*. People deserve to have credit given when credit is due. This also gives your listeners an impression that you are a generous leader who is magnanimous about sharing credit and success. When you tell stories, try to see how many times you can use the word "we" instead of "I."

Use Humor Where Appropriate

There's nothing that people like more than a story that has some observational humor in it. When people laugh at a story, it's a shared experience. They feel better about the speaker, and the story becomes more memorable. However, use great caution; make sure that the humor in the stories is entirely appropriate to the situation and the context. If you're talking about potential layoffs, then humor may not be the most appropriate approach. The classic rules apply when you tell stories: You should not tell any stories that deal with race, religion, culture, or sex, because all you will do is get yourself in trouble.

Focus on Connecting

When you are telling stories from a leadership perspective, in the back of your mind you should ask yourself, "How do I connect with my audience in a way that is unusual and compelling?" When you adopt that mindset, it changes the way you communicate because you're being more "them-centric."

As a leader, if you tell stories repeatedly and consistently, you will develop team pride, raise morale, and improve communication. You'll find that eventually other people on your team start telling the same stories that you tell. This is how you truly start building an amazing and consistent culture.

WORK IT

Do you tell stories about yourself?

_____

_____

_____

_____

_____

Do you tell stories about your team?

_____

_____

_____

_____

_____

Do you believe storytelling can help build culture?

_____

_____

_____

_____

_____

_____

Do you tell stories about your company?

_____

_____

_____

_____

_____

_____

_____

Write down what you need to do in this area. Now create an action plan.

_____

_____

_____

_____

_____

_____

_____

CHAPTER 10

JOLT #10:
ALWAYS BE HONEST
AND AUTHENTIC

*"Honesty is such a lonely word / everyone is so
untrue / Honesty is hardly ever heard / and
mostly what I need from you."*
—BILLY JOEL SONG "HONESTY"

IN this chapter, I am going to address the vital importance
of being both honest and authentic. Why are honesty and
authenticity important? As we have mentioned in several
chapters of this book, the goal of a leader is to get results
from people. The only way this can happen is if you develop
loyalty and trust with the folks who report to you. The only
way to have that loyalty and trust is to be open, honest, and
authentic.

As I often jokingly say when I speak to audiences, every
single person on the planet is born with a very sophisticated
device. This device is often covered in anatomy class at
school, but we somehow missed the lesson. This very small

but sophisticated and sensitive device is located about one inch below the surface of your skin, right around your solar plexus. What is this amazing technological device? I call it a BS alarm! It is the alarm that goes off when someone is "blowing smoke" in your general direction. Can you tell when someone is blowing smoke and not telling you the truth? Yes! Of course you can. By the same token, that means that people can also tell when you are not being real with them. So what does this have to do with this particular chapter? Well, people in the workplace are tired of bosses and managers who are fake, plastic, disingenuous, and only believe in protecting their own self-interest. They try to act as if they care, but it certainly does not work—everyone can tell that they're not being honest and real. They think they can pull it off, but they can't.

Let me provide you with a few real-life examples, with the names changed to protect the innocent. I once worked for an organization where the person I reported to was very disingenuous. Let's call him Zack. When you first met Zack, he appeared to be a very nice and friendly person. However, after working with him for some time, I realized that he was more interested in serving his own needs than mine. The first time I realized this was when I had an article published in an industry journal, *Training and Development Magazine*, which is well known in the training and development community. I went to Zack's office, excited to show him the article. His response was lukewarm at best, and every fiber of my being said that he was actually jealous of my accomplishment because he had not gotten published in this journal first. In other words, I had beaten him to the punch. This showed me that that he was a very insecure individual. On another occasion, Zack asked me to duplicate some videos during my lunch hour. That, I certainly did not mind. I was willing to do my part by working extra hard, and was willing to work through my lunch hour in order to duplicate videos that were a top priority. It wasn't until I began reproducing the videos that I realized I was copying videos of his vacation with his daughter. Why did this project have such urgency? Because the daughter would be flying out of town that day, right after lunch. So the sense of urgency was created, so that she could take the videos with her as she was leaving town. Of course, the ultimate insult was that Zack didn't even thank me for my hard work. He acted as if it had been expected. So, in this case, I had a leader who said that he cared—but the reality was that he only cared when it served his own specific self-interest.

Another manager I worked with, Jess (not his real name), would say one thing and do another. One year I traveled a lot, doing training programs on the road for over 42 weeks during the year. I approached Jess and told him that the workload was entirely too much. I was traveling too much, and I was quite frankly getting burnt out. I told him I didn't think that I would be able to do the same workload the following year. His reply, which was somewhat shocking, was, "Well, don't you realize how lucky you are that you get to travel all over the country and see amazing sights?" Yes, that was true; I got to see the "sites" on the way from the airport to the hotel and back. I was in those towns working and doing training—obviously, I did not get to see any of the sites. I was not on vacation. Again he said he cared, but his commentary on my dilemma was so flippant and uncaring that it was a shock and conflicted with his overarching message. I also noticed that this leader would treat women who were attractive much differently than he treated everyone else. When I called him on this behavior, he denied it while at the same time looking embarrassed and humiliated.

When we lack authenticity, we will find that our team is less loyal and less supportive, and employees will not spend a lot of time in our department before transferring somewhere else in the organization.

How do leaders ensure that they are being honest and authentic? Here are five areas that you might want to truly consider as you develop a foundation for this particular thought process:

Know Who You Are

What does that mean? What it means is that you have a specific and unique personality and style. Most likely, you have had a similar personality and style your entire life. Sure, you have spent some time refining and polishing, developing your strengths and eliminating some of your weaknesses, but the reality is that there are certain core principles that you have. These are core principles that you cannot and should not abandon. You have certain ethical beliefs, professional beliefs, and other thoughts about how things should be run. Your belief about how things should be run is probably based on your personal value system. Unfortunately, when some people move to another company or a new culture, they feel as if they cannot be who they are, or they will not fit in with the specific culture of their new organization. If you feel as if you have to be different from the person that you are in order to fit in with your organization as a leader, then I would strongly urge you to consider working somewhere else. If you have a significant philosophical difference with your current employer, that is not a good feeling.

Take Some Assessments

As mentioned in an earlier chapter, one way of learning more about who you are is to take some specific assessments that are available online or on paper. There are leadership assessments, behavioral style assessments (such as DISC, the Platinum Rule, MBTI, and so on), listening assessments, and communication style assessments, just to name a few. Each time you take a specific assessment, you will learn more about yourself as a person and as a leader. These specific assessments will give you objective feedback about your strengths and your weaknesses, as well as areas for improvement. Let's say that you take a behavioral styles assessment that indicates you are a high-energy social person. This identification of your particular style reinforces what you may or may not already believe about yourself. The value of this particular tool is that you will now understand why you react the way you do in specific situations, both at work and at home. The bottom line is that assessments help you gain a better understanding of who you are. I also suggest that you share the results of your various assessments with significant people in your life, to help them validate the results for you. The discussions that you share with people in your personal life about these assessments can also deepen your understanding of the assessment results. Sometimes when I give this advice, people say, "Well, I would like to take those assessments, but my company won't pay for them." So? Just because your company does not pay for it, doesn't mean you shouldn't do it anyway and pay for the expense out of your own pocket. The more knowledge you gain about yourself, the better off you will be. It will also make you a more effective leader.

Know What You Believe In

Take some quiet time, sit down at your desk with a blank legal pad, and write down a series of statements about what you believe in. In this list you might write, "I believe in hard work, and I believe there is significant reward for hard work, and I believe that everyone on the planet should be treated in a humane fashion." Your list of "I believe" statements will crystallize what you already know. These are the core concepts that you believe in.

Note Your Strengths

If you asked 10 people you know to list your specific professional strengths, what would they say? The second question is, would their answers be the same as your answers? This certainly is an interesting question. The goal behind understanding your strengths is that you can be very open and honest about them. Additionally, you can also be open and honest about the areas that are not your strengths. Some people in leadership roles assume that it is a mistake to admit having weaknesses. The truth is the opposite—it's a strength to know them.

Make a Commitment to the Truth

This is obviously a personal decision as well as a professional one, but I believe that people in a leadership position should be committed to telling the truth 100 percent of the time. Why is this important? As a person in a leadership role, telling people something that is not true is doing them a grave disservice. Why? Because they trust that you are being honest and they will then leave the conversation or transaction believing something that is false. Let me give you an example. Let's say one of your team members gets up in front of a group and gives a presentation, including PowerPoint and handouts. As you are observing the presentation, it gradually dawns on you that the team member doing the presentation is doing a truly awful job. After the presentation is over, and everyone has left, you say to the person, "Wow, Cindy, that was a really good presentation, and I appreciate all your hard work." Cindy then leaves the room assuming that you told her the truth, and the reality is that you didn't. What you should say instead is, "I really appreciate the hard work you put into the presentation, but I don't feel today that it really got the results that we were looking for." Then you could have a conversation about what went well and what could be improved. This conversation would actually be truthful and would help Cindy grow and develop her presentation skills. You can tell people the truth and still be diplomatic and careful in the way you position it, so that it is not offensive. They may not enjoy hearing the news, but they will respect you for being honest.

Now you understand the key concepts of Leadership. Now what? Go out there and be the kind of leader who inspires, motivates, and truly makes a difference in our world. Make it happen!

I hope you enjoyed this book.

Shawn Doyle is a motivational speaker, author, trainer, consultant, and business coach. He is available to provide the following services:

Speaking at your next meeting
Training on sales, motivation, or leadership
Custom training
Executive coaching
Life coaching
Sales coaching

If you would like to contact Shawn with questions or comments, send Shawn an e-mail at
SLDoyle1@aol.com

Visit Shawn's website for free articles and other resources:
www.sldoyle.com

ABOUT SHAWN DOYLE, CSP

Shawn Doyle is a learning and development professional who has a passion for human potential. He is an avid believer in the concept of lifelong learning. For the last 23 years, Shawn has spent his time developing and implementing training programs on team-building, communication, creativity, motivation, and leadership. He is the author of 14 books, and a Certified Speaking Professional. (Only 8 percent of speakers in the world are CSPs.)

Shawn's company helps people become more effective in the workplace and in their lives. His clients include Pfizer, Comcast, Charter Media, IBM, Kraft, Microsoft, the US Marines, the Ladders, and Los Alamos National Defense Laboratory.

JUMPSTART
your
LEADERSHIP NOTES

_____
_____
_____
_____
_____
_____
_____
_____
_____
_____
_____
_____
_____
_____
_____
_____
_____
_____
_____
_____